DECOYS

NORTH AMERICA'S ONE HUNDRED GREATEST

Loy S. Harrell Jr.

Published by

**krause
publications**

The World's Largest Hobby & Collectibles Publisher

700 E. State St.
Iola, WI 54990-0001
Telephone 715-445-2214
www.krause.com

Please call or write for our free catalog. Our toll-free number to place an order or obtain a free catalog is 800-258-0929 or please use our regular business telephone 715-445-2214 for editorial comment and further information.

Library of Congress Catalog Number: 00-102684

ISBN: 0-87341-921-9

Printed in Canada

Acknowledgments

It is with great appreciation and gratitude that I list the following names. Without their assistance and guidance this book would not have materialized. All are noted decoy collectors and/or dealers. When I asked for help in listing the great decoys and their whereabouts, these people responded; Donna and Joseph Tonelli, John Delph, Gary Guyette, James Doherty, Joe Engers, Alan Haid, Russ Goldberger, Larry Pollin, Vance Strausburg, Donal O'Brien Jr., John Proctor, Ted Harmon, Dick McIntyre, Frank Schmidt, Steve Miller, James Cook, Jackson Parker, James Allen, Ronald Swanson, Joe French, Bobby Richardson and Gigi Hopkins.

Further assistance was freely given by David Wise and William Stanton, who respectively designed and photographed the jacket; Jane Beck, Curator of the Vermont Folklife Museum, Middlebury, Vermont; Robin Woodworth, photograph collection manager, Shelburne Museum, Shelburne, Vermont; Rae Harrell, for her typing and artistic skills; Gloria Reynolds for her work on the cover; Lance Povlock for his computer expertise; the patient and tireless trio of Cynthia Stokes, Katherine Smith and Mary Ann Cootware who worked with me for eighteen months in processing and developing my photographs. Photographic Plates #24, 26, 148, 170, and 192, courtesy of Robert Gerard, Donna Tonelli, Douglas Ashley, David Fischer and Joseph French respectively.

Eight decoys in this book are from the collection of Dr. James McCleery. I had the privilege of spending a full day with Dr. McCleery, photographing his decoys, making doctor talk and trading decoy anecdotes. Sadly, Dr. McCleery recently passed away and his famous collection was auctioned to the public. Many new world price records were achieved, both for individual carvers and decoys per se. As a tribute to Dr. McCleery, each of his decoys appearing in the book will be marked; "Collection of James McCleery, M.D." and the new owner will be designated by an asterisk[*].

Also thanks to my sidekick and companion, Malcolm, the best four-legged friend a man could have. You will find his picture in this book.

Loy S. Harrell Jr.

Dedication

This book is in memory of my father,
Loy Sherman Harrell Sr.
He would have said, "Good work, son!"

Contents

Foreword 6
Introduction 7
Humpback Pintails by Lem and Steve Ward 8
Wood Duck by Thomas Chambers 10
Redhead Drake by Nathan Cobb Jr. 12
Widgeon Drake by Stevens Decoy Factory 14
Sleeping Swan by Charles "Shang" Wheeler 16
Rig of Green-wing Teals by Clovis "Cadice" Vizier 18
Preening Black Duck by Elmer Crowell 20
Red-breasted Merganser by Captain Edwin
    Backman .22
Red-breasted Mergansers by an unknown maker 24
Great Blue Heron by an unknown maker 26
Green-winged Teal by John Blair Sr. 28
Oldsquaws by Joseph Lincoln 30
Hooded Merganser Drake by Orel LeBoeuf 32
Shoveler Hen by Lem and Steve Ward 34
Preening Mallard Hen by Robert Elliston 36
Redhead Drake by Harry V. Shourds Sr. 38
Red-breasted Mergansers by Lloyd Parker 40
Monhegan Island Eider Drake by Augustus Wilson . . .42
Canvasbacks by Lem and Steve Ward 44
Black Duck by Albert D. Laing 46
Short-billed Dowitcher by Obediah Verity 48
Ruddy Duck by Lee Dudley 50
Canada Goose by Charles Walker 52
Canvasback Hen by Albert D. Laing 54
Canada Goose by the Warin Brothers 56
Brant by Nathan Cobb Jr. 58
Pintail Drake by Charles Walker 60
Mallard Drake by Nicole Vidacovich Sr. 62
Sickle-billed Curlew by an unknown maker 64
Hissing Goose by Nathan Cobb Jr. 66
Wood Duck Drake by Joseph Lincoln 68
Merganser Hen by George Boyd 70
Shorebird Rig by Harry V. Shourds Sr. 72
Merganser Drake by Cassius Smith 74

Snow Goose by John Tax 76
Pair of Whimbrels by William Bowman 78
Canada Goose and Pintail Drake by Elmer Crowell . .80
Curlew by an unknown maker 82
Mallard Drake by the Caines Brothers 84
Herring Gull by Harry V. Shourds Sr. 86
Canada Goose by Henry Kilpatrick 88
Wood Duck Drakes, Premier Grade, by the Mason
    Company .90
Green-winged Teals by Elmer Crowell 92
Pintails by Dave "Umbrella" Watson 94
Canada Goose by Nathan Cobb Jr. 96
Black-bellied Plover by Elmer Crowell 98
Swan by an unknown maker 100
Merganser Drake by Captain Charles G. Osgood . . .102
Pintail Drake Ice Duck by Charles
    Schoenheider Sr. 104
Canada Goose by George Boyd 106
American Merganser by an unknown maker 108
Widgeon Drake Preener by Elmer Crowell 110
Rig of Mergansers by an unknown maker 112
Green-winged Teal Drake by Charles Perdew 114
Canada Goose by Joseph Lincoln 116
Canvasbacks by John Graham 118
Pintail Drake by Lem and Steve Ward 120
Canada Goose by Enoch Reindahl 122
Pintail Drake by John Blair Sr. 124
Canvasback Drake Preener by Elmer A. Crowell . . .126
Black Duck Sleeper by Robert Elliston 128
Merganser Hen by John Dawson 130
Mallard Hen by Charles Perdew 132
Eskimo Curlews by the Folger Family 134
Eider Drake by an unknown maker 136
Pintail Hen by John English 138
Mallard Drake Ice Duck by Charles
    Schoenheider Sr. 140
Mallard Hen by Nathan R. Horner 142

Curlew by Thomas Gelston 144
Canvasback Hen by Charles "Shang" Wheeler 146
Black Brant by William McLellan 148
Canada Goose by Captain Charles G. Osgood 150
Buffleheads by Nathan R. Horner 152
Brant by Chauncey M. Wheeler 154
Canada Goose by Walter Brady 156
Mallard Drake by Shang Wheeler 158
American Widgeon by Lem and Steve Ward 160
Red-breasted Merganser by Augustus Wilson 162
Mallard Hen Sleeper by Charles Perdew 164
Swan by Charles Birch 166
Canada Goose by Elmer Crowell 168
Black-bellied Plover by John Dilley 170
Hooded Mergansers by Ira Hudson 172
Bishop's Head Goose by Lem and Steve Ward 174
Canada Goose by an unknown maker 176
Widgeon Drake by John Blair Sr. 178
Mallard Hen by the Caines Brothers 180
Black-bellied Plover by Obediah Verity 182
Canada Goose Ice Decoy by Charles
    Schoenheider Sr. 184
Hudsonian Curlew by William Bowman 186
Canada Goose by Harry V. Shourds Sr. 188
Swan by Albert D. Laing 190
Canada Goose by Phineas Reeves 192
Curlew by Nathan Cobb Jr. 194
Mallard Drake by Victor Alfonso 196
Swan by John "Daddy" Holly 198
Curlew by John Verity 200
Ruddy Turnstone by Lothrop Holmes 202
Widgeon Drake by Nathan Horner 204
Pintail Drake by John English/John Dawson 206

Index 208

Foreword

When Loy told me about his plans for a book about the one hundred greatest decoys and asked for my cooperation in this venture, I jumped at the chance for three reasons: (1) It was about time we had such a "Hall of Fame" list, (2) It would be in Loy's capable hands, backed up by some very knowledgeable collectors and dealers, and (3) It would be done by someone else, not me, so I wouldn't be awakened after midnight by an irate Californian who would berate me for leaving out "Fresh Air Dick."

It would not be the first time I've been involved in such a decoy rating enterprise, but my previous two rating experiences fell short of the scope of Loy's effort.

I thought I had a valid rating of greatness when I originated the Highest-Price Lots at Decoy Auctions in the annual reviews of The Decoy at Auction in *Decoy Magazine*. After all, I reasoned, isn't this rating by cost a legitimate measurement of greatness; collectors backing up their opinions with cold hard cash? Not quite, because some of the great decoys in museums and/or private collections have never come to auction and some that had come to auction have done so long ago when prices were still low.

And in June 1981, when sixteen of us assembled at the Shelburne Museum in Vermont to evaluate the greatest collection of wildfowl decoys in the world, we voted on their five most important decoys, and this is how it came out:

First: Lee Dudley (VA) ruddy duck

Second: Shang Wheeler (CT) mallard pair

Third: (tie) John Blair Sr. (MD/PA) pintail and William Bowman (ME/NY) shorebirds

Fifth: (tie) Thomas Gelston (NY) curlews, Mason factory (MI) curlews and Charles Osgood (MA) geese

It was a formal rating by sixteen knowledgeable collectors but limited to the Shelburne decoys. What is significant is that all the above decoys or their rigmates in other collections, except the Wheeler mallard hen and Mason curlews, turned up on Loy's One Hundred Greatest. Only four of us voted in both formal ratings eighteen years apart, which indicates some consistency of standards in judging what makes the best of our classic decoys.

I expected a good solid list including some of my favorite decoys. I expected some of my favorites among the missing. What I did not expect were some classics I never knew existed and the splendor of Loy's big photos.

In my library of more than sixty books about decoys, plus many auction catalogues and periodicals on the subject, appear many of the classic decoys on Loy's list. Now we have the one hundred greatest in one book. What a pleasure it will be for the old-time collector to renew acquaintance with classics he may have had contact with at auctions, shows or other collections. And how helpful it will be to the novice who will get an education in judging standards just by turning the pages in this book. It took a great deal of work to get this book through to its final stage, and from what I have seen in the advanced proofs, the decoy collecting fraternity will find it eminently worthwhile.

Jackson Parker
Honorary Curator of Wildlife Decoys
Peabody Essex Museum
Salem, Massachusetts

Introduction

What is it like to orbit planet earth or land on the moon? Take it from me, no easy task; at least that is my educated perspective. What is it like to find, photograph and chronicle the top one hundred decoys of North America? Need I again make the comparison? To equate the latter feat to landing on the moon is obviously far-fetched. However, in a relative fashion, if I had asked Neil Armstrong to trade places, he no doubt would have opted for his now famous adventure.

Since no one has attempted this before, the concept must be a difficult one. *The Great Book of Wildfowl Decoys* by Joe Engers documents many great decoys, some of which I photographed for this book. However, it doesn't go out on a limb to select the top one hundred. *Decoys, North America's One Hundred Greatest*, does in fact make this leap. It also is a mechanism by which many top decoys will be viewed that have heretofore never been seen, and much less, photographed.

Why this book? Obviously, as I stated, it was a challenge. But most of all it was done because it should be done. Decoys have become one of North America's most favorite and prestigious collectibles. Their folk art appeal, inherent monetary value and rarity all combine to put decoys at or near the top of the list as the most sought-after pieces of collectible art. Resultantly, a great wealth of knowledge about decoying and their carvers has emerged; all adding to the lore and attractiveness of this art form.

My next step was to ask a great number of collectors to list what they considered to be the top twenty or thirty decoys. I had an almost immediate response. Their reaction enhanced my sense that I was on a subject that most collectors were excited about. The top one-hundred! What are they and who has them? After several months of research and subsequent phone calls, I spent most of 1998 and 1999 hop-scotching around North America photographing and documenting more than two hundred and fifty exceptional decoys. To be specific, when I say decoys, I am referring to ducks, shorebirds and geese which were carved and used for hunting between the mid 19th and the mid 20th centuries.

The selection process was influenced by general consensus of collectors, rarity of the decoy, condition, geographic consideration, provenance or maker, and perhaps its unusual eye appeal or form. I was most fortunate in that I knew most of the noted collectors whose decoys I photographed. Admittedly, I was often overwhelmed by the uniqueness and beauty of these collections. I had a ball! All photographs were taken out-of-doors to create an artistic setting to preclude a sense of sterility in the format.

To give due respect to this effort and not to be presumptuous, I enlisted the help of eight very knowledgeable decoy collectors. Each was asked to select his or her top one hundred from the decoys I had photographed. A compilation was made and this book represents those selected. As an exercise in literary license, I chose to include more than one decoy in several photographs, such as pairs or a rig of decoys in an effort to make a salient point. There is no specific order, i.e. one is not considered more important than the other. In addition to the author the following people were on this select committee; Joseph and Donna Tonelli, Lake Andes, South Dakota; Gary Guyette, Farmington, Maine; Joseph Engers, Lewes, Delaware; Alan Haid, Darien, Connecticut; Russ Goldberger, Hampton, New Hampshire; James Allen, Tuckerton, New Jersey and John Southworth, St. Paul, Minnesota.

I hope all enjoy this book. However, I have one request of the reader; don't call and tell me about the one I missed! I realize it's inevitable.

Loy S. Harrell Jr.
Hinesburg, Vermont
February 1, 2000

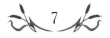

Humpback Pintails

by Lem (1896-1984) and Steve (1895-1976) Ward, Chrisfield, Maryland

Pintails, or sprigtails, were abundant along the lower portion of the Eastern Shore. This area encompasses the lower part of Maryland and Virginia including much of Chesapeake Bay. The pintail, along with the goldeneye, does not easily decoy into rigs of other species. Therefore, there was a great demand for the Wards to produce this lure. It is said to be the favorite bird of Lem; which is exemplified by his special effort to paint the pintail in stylish and vivid colors. This pair of exquisite Humpback decoys are typical of the mid-1920s period; a time that can truly be said to be the "folksy" period. They have original paint, heads that virtually rest on the body, stunning long upswept tails and rotund bodies; a rare and unique example of American folk art. Each reader should make an effort to visit the Ward Museum of Wildfowl Art in Salisbury, Maryland where a variety of great Ward decoys are on exhibit. The museum, built in 1992, at a cost of $5 million is a magnificent structure which houses one of the greatest collections of waterfowl carvings in the country.

Collection of Lloyd Griffith, M.D.

Wood Duck

by Thomas Chambers (1864-1950), Toronto, Canada

The confluence of Lake Huron, Lake Ontario, Lake Erie and Lake St. Clair has always been one of the most prolific duck hunting areas in North America. Flocks of thousands of ducks and geese migrate through this area from the Canadian Prairies and as far away as Hudson Bay and the Arctic. In the 1800s it was a Mecca for the market gunner and for wealthy sportsmen throughout Canada and the United States. In his early years Chambers was also a market gunner and guide for members of the St. Anne's Club on Lake St. Clair. After a fire razed the St. Anne's Club in 1900, Chambers became manager for the next forty years of the St. Clair Flats Shooting Company. Chambers' decoys are especially graceful lures; hollow with a first curve of the neck from the same block of wood as the body. From the early 1900s to today, Chambers' decoys are cherished by the collector. This wood duck is extremely rare and was carved circa 1900-1910.

Private Collection

Redhead Drake

by Nathan Cobb Jr. (1825-1905), Cobb Island, Virginia

Cobb Island Resort was a vacationers' Mecca during the Victorian period of the 19th century. Tourists and guests would arrive by rail to the coast and be ferried by boat to enjoy the ambiance of the island. Room and meals were advertised for $3 per day or $18 per week. The Cobbs ran a very successful enterprise, which was an endeavor of all the children and their families. Associated with this setting was, of course, a great abundance of waterfowl. Market gunning was at its peak and the tables of the hotel must have been overflowing with wonderful home-cooked meals harvested from the sea. As waterfowl became more wary of the gunners, there became a need for carved lures. The Cobbs were up to this task, making geese, black ducks, bluebills, brants, redheads and shorebirds. This redhead drake is a fine example of a Cobb diver, hollow with carved eyes and inletted head. This decoy is photographed on the water north of Oyster, Virginia.

Collection of Grayson and Dawn Chesser

Widgeon Drake

by Stevens Decoy Factory, Weedsport, New York

Harvey A. Stevens, born in 1847, lived on the fringe of the great Montezuma Swamp, now a National Wildlife Refuge. He became a market gunner and resultantly began carving his own decoys. His lures were aesthetically pleasing as well as functional and were in demand by other hunters. In 1880, Stevens established the Stevens Decoy Factory. In that year he advertised nationally in *Forest And Stream* magazine and soon was shipping his decoys around the country. His business, assisted by brothers George and Fred, continued until Harvey's death in 1894. Stevens' decoys are beautifully painted and

Harvey stated in his literature, "In painting, nothing but the best paint is used; and for style and neatness they are unsurpassed." Any collector would vouch for this appraisal. The widgeon pictured here is the round-bottom style, which Harvey found to ride better in the water. Each decoy has two recessed 7/8-inch holes in the bottom; one for lead ballast and the other for a staple to secure the anchor line. This particular decoy is marked G.W. Stevens, Weedsport, New York, Manufacturer, Standard Decoy.

Collection of Lloyd Griffith, M.D.

Sleeping Swan

by Charles "Shang" Wheeler (1872-1949), Stratford, Connecticut

"Shang" was Connecticut's most famous decoy maker. He was also a noted civic leader and politician; serving in the Connecticut House and Senate for three terms. Later he served six years as Commissioner of Fisheries and Game for the state. Wheeler was large in stature and got his nickname for the P. T. Barnum circus giant named "Chang." It was a nickname that lasted throughout Wheeler's lifetime. In Wheeler's youth he became a market gunner and made many decoys for his own use. His style was after Albert Laing, the father of the "Stratford School" makers. In later years he began to make more refined decoys such as this swan. These were his show-quality lures. His ability and creativity had a far-reaching and national influence on decoy carving and collecting. Wheeler entered many national contests and was invariably a blue ribbon winner. His decoys are highly prized by collectors.

Collection of James and Diane Cook

Rig of Green-winged Teals

by Clovis "Cadice" Vizier (1879-1976), Galliano, Louisiana

The area known as Bayou Laforche has long been one of Louisiana's primary waterways, linking the Mississippi River with the Gulf of Mexico. Clovis Vizier, his father Beauregard (1840-1934), and brother Odee (1892-1969), were all noted Bayou Laforche carvers. They supplied decoys to both the "Sport" and the market gunner. This rig of teals exemplifies the mastery of Clovis' carving skills; constructed of either tupelo gum or cypress, each was hand-chopped and honed with a knife; then painted in a skillful manner. In 1951 Clovis entered a pair of mallards in the North American Decoy Makers contest in New York City, taking a second place. When one referred to Clovis they paid high tribute by saying, "Cadice, he knew the birds." Unfortunately in 1965 Hurricane Betsy, which passed over much of the Gulf, destroyed the drake mallard along with many other decoys from the Vizier family.

Collection of Brian and Emilie Cheramie

Preening Black Duck

by Elmer Crowell (1862-1952) Harwich, Massachusetts

It seems that this collector's decoys, for the majority, are not looking where they are going. That is, many are sleepers and preeners. Significantly, these forms demand higher prices at auction and are more desirable for collectors. This particular black duck is truly an expression of Crowell's artistic skill. He must have enjoyed creating this form; for a significant number of his more beautiful decoys are sleepers or preeners. Note the raised and crossed wing tips, which is consistent with Crowell's early (1900-1915) work. Black ducks are predominately an East Coast species. Their flyway encompasses the East and Midwest regions of North America. Hence, a great preponderance of black duck decoys are by East Coast carvers. It is worth noting that puddle ducks, including the black duck, have made a resurgence in numbers due to the use of steel shot. Ingestion of lead pellets was lethal to these species.

Private California Collection

Red-breasted Merganser

by Captain Edwin Backman (1872-1914), Lunnenburg, Nova Scotia

Backman was an offshore fisherman and captain of a cargo schooner out of Lunnenburg. He had a strong knowledge of the sea and grew up as a hunter and carver of decoys. The South Shore of Nova Scotia was a fine haven for migrating ducks, marked by deep bays and marshes. This afforded Backman the apparent opportunity to carve and perfect this beautiful lure. Flowing lines, muted intricate paint, upswept tails and delicate crests characterize his mergansers. This merganser is the only one of this style in original paint.

It is also pictured on page 69 of *Decoys Of Maritime Canada*, by Gary and Dale Guyette. At the outbreak of World War I, Backman set sail in his three-masted schooner, the "William Cortada" for the West Indies. Backman told friends that he thought the Schooner was poorly designed and that it would "...be the death of me." He was apparently correct, for he was never heard from again.

Collection of Gary and Dale Guyette

Red-breasted Mergansers

by an unknown maker, Barnegat Bay, New Jersey, circa 1920

Mergansers are the fastest flying duck. Clocked at one hundred mph, (versus the teal at forty mph) they were an elusive target and gunners expended many shells attempting to shoot this streamlined bird. Fortunately for the mergansers, today virtually no one decoys or shoots this species. Therefore finding a fine pair of early working merganser decoys is a plus for any collector. These birds are branded "J.S.L." for Joseph Lippincott. He was a sportsman and publisher who resided in Philadelphia, Pennsylvania. The collector has been unable to establish whether Lippincott was the carver or merely branded these decoys to identify them as his own. Historically, we know that Lippincott gave decoys to the Shelburne Museum, including a Mason wood duck. The pictured decoys are fine examples of a New Jersey carving; hollow, padded lead weights and made strictly for hunting.

Collection of Robert Jr. and Wilma Gerard

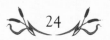

Great Blue Heron

by an unknown maker, Crane Lake Gun Club, Bath, Illinois

This particular wading bird is perhaps one of the most wary of all species. By its very nature, the great blue heron relies on stealth and silence to find its quarry. Any disturbance causes the heron to be distracted and flee. These characteristics make them an ideal confidence decoy. Some gunners would use one or two herons for each stool of decoys. Heron habitats are marshy shorelines of ponds, lakes and coastal waters. Therefore, migrating waterfowl are familiar with this wading bird and feel a sense of safety in their presence. Only a few of these rare decoys have survived from the early 1900s. Several have been found on Long Island, New York and a particularly beautiful one by Cornelius Barkelow of Barnegat, New Jersey, is in the William Mackey family collection. Their size and fragility were factors against longevity. The heron shown here is an exceptional piece of sculpture. It has an inserted walnut bill and multiple inserted copper tail feathers. The maker took extra measures to create not only a functional decoy, but also a thing of beauty.

Collection of Joseph and Donna Tonelli

Green-winged Teal

by John Blair Sr. (1842-1928) Philadelphia, Pennsylvania

The workmanship and paint of decoys carved by John Blair Sr. are unparalleled. Historically, researchers have discovered a link between Blair, a wheelwright, and his "friend" a trolley painter. Their mutual interest in duck hunting and perhaps market gunning lead them to artistically create, perhaps hundreds of gunning lures. Blair decoys have been found throughout the United States and there are at least one hundred known in collections. The "classic" styles are hollow, have round bottoms and the halves are pinned with dowels. "Second grade" are hollow but with flat bottoms and "third grade" decoys are solid body. Paint style is consistent which leads to the conclusion that the "trolley man" painted them all. Blair decoys have a raised neck shelf and this peculiarity is a must for a true Blair. The photographed teal is an example of the "classic style." It is pictured on page 33 of *Floating Sculpture* by Doug Knight and H. Harrison Huster.

Collection of Bruce Williams

Oldsquaws

by Joseph Lincoln (1859-1938), Accord, Massachusetts

When we refer to the great decoy makers, Joe Lincoln is always among them. Early in his teens, Lincoln observed waterfowl on Accord Pond across from his home. They became his passion and soon his vocation. Lincoln was known throughout the Cape as one of two major producers of duck decoys; the other being Elmer Crowell. Lincoln's rigs were very innovative but simple in style and paint. He made "loomers," large slat geese to attract high-flying flocks, self-bailing decoys, all species of ducks and wonderful miniatures. Using advertising as an avenue for work, Lincoln soon became one of the most prolific carvers on the East Coast. He carved well into his seventies and was listed in the 1930 Hingham phone directory as "Joseph Lincoln, Age 70, Decoy Maker." A complete line of decoys was offered for sale including black ducks, geese, scoters, oldsquaws, goldeneyes, brant and mergansers. Oldsquaws are primarily confined to coastal waters. There, its natural food supply of shrimp, small fish, and mollusks is abundant. They are one of the very few diving ducks that propel themselves with their wings when underwater. They have the ability to dive to great depths; as deep as eighty fathoms. This pair of Lincoln oldsquaws represent some of his finest painting.

Private Collection

Hooded Merganser Drake

by Orel LeBoeuf (1886-1968), St. Anicet, Quebec, Canada

Recognized early in his life as a prolific and true decoy artist, LeBoeuf's lures were elusive and difficult to find. He led a reclusive lifestyle; often holing up in a diminutive ice-fishing hut heated by a hanging oil lamp. LeBoeuf was one of Canada's early market gunners. Traveling to Ontario each fall he would bivouac on a small island and shoot ducks over his own decoys. When he had accumulated 200 to 300 birds, he would return to Montreal to sell his take. To his benefit, he was very particular with his carvings.

Only the best paint and distinctive details were put into his decoys, therefore making a LeBoeuf sculpture a truly fine addition to any collection. The merganser pictured here, without question, is the finest of all known LeBoeufs. This decoy is pictured in a number of publications including *The Great Book Of Wildfowl Decoys* by Joe Engers.

Collection of Jamie Stalker

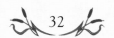

Shoveler Hen

by Lem (1896-1984) and Steve (1895-1976) Ward, Chrisfield, Maryland

Ward aficionados will argue whether this decoy is a working cedar lure or a decorative piece. The author has heard both sides, as has the collector. However the preponderance of opinion leads to that of the working or gunning variety. This is without question, one-of-a-kind for the Wards. If there is a drake to pair up with this lovely hen, I'm sure the collector would like to know it. The Wards made shoveler decoys as mostly decorative pieces. These were usually hollow cedar with raised wing tips. In contrast, the shoveler hen pictured here is solid cedar and constructed like other Ward gunning decoys. It has a spectacular paint pattern that expresses Lem Ward at his finest. Characteristically this form and construction are consistent with the late 1930s. Shovelers are seldom seen on the East Coast, accounting for the rarity of shoveler decoys. Their range is primarily from British Columbia, south to Mexico. Because it often feeds in stagnant ponds, it is particularly susceptible to botulism, a fatal bacterial food poisoning.

Collection of Alan and Elaine Haid

Preening Mallard Hen

by Robert Elliston (1849-1915), Bureau, Illinois

I n the fall of 1990 I was present at a duck hunting camp on the coast of Maine along with auction promoter Gary Guyette and the present owner of this circa 1890 Elliston mallard. Guyette had the decoy tucked away and at the opportune moment displayed it at the dinner table. We were awed! A Wisconsin antique dealer found it for $75 at a house tag sale. We wanted to buy it on the spot. The bidding reached $20,000; however Guyette was obligated to put it into the April 1991 auction in Chicago. There the collector had to up his ante to a world record for an Elliston

decoy. The mallard is branded "Dupee," who was a wealthy sportsman who hunted the Horicon Marsh in the late 1800s. Elliston was a commercial decoy maker and the first to make sleepers or preening lures. The paint was laid on by his wife Catherine. Without question, Elliston set the precedent for fine, hollow Illinois River decoys. His contemporaries followed in his path and continued what is now called the Illinois River School.

Private California Collection

Redhead Drake

by Harry V. Shourds Sr. (1861-1920), Tuckerton, New Jersey

John Hillman and Lloyd Johnson, two noted New Jersey carvers and collectors, collaborated and found a rig of seven Shourds decoys. All were redheads made circa 1890-1900 and branded J.E.B. These were reported to come from the family of James E. Baines, who had resided in Washington, D. C. Baines was a noted carver and guide on the Susquehanna River and the Western Shore of Maryland. It has not been determined if the J.E.B. brand was Baines Sr. or Baines Jr. Nevertheless, these decoys are in dry, mint condition and never touched salt water. All are now in famous collections. This particular redhead is from the Malcolm Fleming collection and so signed. Further, it was the subject of a waterfowl painting by nationally noted artist Burton Moore Jr.

Collection of James and Debra Allen

Red-breasted Mergansers

by Lloyd Parker (1859-1921), Parkertown, New Jersey

Parker, a Barnegat Bay bayman, fisherman and decoy carver was from an enclave just north of Tuckerton, New Jersey. Here he made hundreds of decoys for the area gunners and sportsmen. It is recorded in 1912 that he sold a dozen black ducks for $7. Since duck hunting during this period was at its zenith, demand for carved working rigs was great. Parker helped to fill this void. His decoys personify the Barnegat Bay style; very light weight, thinly hollow bodies with inletted lead ballast and with the typical ice groove behind the head. The paint style is simple yet elegant and functional. These beautiful mergansers, circa 1900, were put on the shelf by the Parker family and were never weighted. They eventually became an important part of the John Hillman collection. At auction in 1996, they were described in the catalog as the "finest pair of birds to come out of the state of New Jersey" and were sold for $132,000; a record for a Parkertown decoy.

Collection of Cameron and Jean Troilo

Monhegan Island Eider Drake

by Augustus Wilson (1864-1950), South Portland, Maine

More than fifty years of carving decoys and the creation of five thousand lures has made Wilson one of the most famous of all carvers. His influence on Maine Coast carvers is legion. Most of Wilson's adult life was spent as a fisherman and as a lighthouse attendant; the last job being the keeper of Spring Point Light in Casco Bay, Maine. This latter employment gave him ample time to carve his now-famous rigs. From turned heads, preeners, sleepers, rocking heads to the swivel-head styles, he was the master. Carved eyes, raised carved wings and inletted heads typify Wilson's decoys. The Monhegan style is his earliest, dating from 1890 to 1910. These are characterized by large bold forms as seen in this eider drake. Wilson is also known to have shipped decoys to Monhegan Island where this decoy was found. Eiders were hunted in the 19th century, primarily for their down. For hundreds of years, down had been gathered from nests in Northern Europe and used to make pillows and quilts. In North America, this practice ended at the turn of the century and there has been a spectacular increase of eiders along the Maine coast. Their survival is now assured. This beautiful decoy was photographed in Central Park, New York City.

Collection of Steve Miller

Canvasbacks

by Lem (1896-1984) and Steve (1895-1976) Ward, Chrisfield, Maryland

Alan Haid, a noted collector, after seeing this pair of Ward carvings circa 1925 said, "These are statement decoys." Meaning first, a cursory glance says they are Wards; secondly, they were carved in the era representing the zenith of the Wards' creative ability, and thirdly, canvasbacks represent the "Species of the Chesapeake Bay," the primary wintering grounds for this majestic duck. Probably 90 percent of the quarry of market gunners were canvasbacks. At the peak of the market hunting era, more than ten thousand were killed each day on the Bay. It is no wonder that the canvasback is now a threatened species. This pair of very rare decoys have unique raised and carved wings. They are signed by the Wards and inscribed on the bottom is a notation that they were made for Weslie Dize, a politician from Chrisfield. These decoys are pictured in several publications including *Ward Brothers Decoys* by Ronald J. Gard and Brian J. McGrath and color plate, page 180, of *Chesapeake Bay Decoys* by Robert H. Richardson. The photograph of these decoys was taken in front of the Ward homestead in Chrisfield, Maryland.

Collection of Loy and Rae Harrell

Black Duck

by Albert D. Laing (1811-1886), New York City and Stratford, Connecticut

Albert Laing was an innovator in decoy carving. His days as a market gunner on Great South Bay and the East River necessitated the use of a large number of decoys. Records he left when he died in 1886 include important historical data about his life. He recorded that during the 1835 season he shot six hundred and eighty three ducks, mostly from his "battery." His market gunning took him to the Chesapeake Bay and the waters of the Delaware River. Laing had relatives in Philadelphia and often traveled there to hunt ducks on the river. Decoys discovered in this location are considered "middle period" carvings and date from 1840 to 1850. They are hollow, graceful lures made for swift water. It was on these decoys that he perfected the scratch painting of the heads that is so typical of the "Stratford School." Without question, Laing was the founder of that style which was perpetuated by successive generations of Stratford makers. Laing always strove to create in his artistry; sleepers, preeners, upright heads and swimmers. His "battery" or wing ducks are no doubt the prototypes for all other such carvings during the 19th and 20th centuries. This elegant black duck from the Delaware River is Laing at his best.

Collection of Lloyd Griffith, M.D.

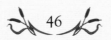

Short-billed Dowitcher

by Obediah Verity (1813-1901), Massapequa, New York

This pristine decoy is one of four found in a Long Island home in 1995. Included were an Eskimo curlew and a long-billed curlew, the former an extinct species. Dowitchers, both long- and short-billed, are large shorebirds, twelve plus inches in length. They fly in groups of thousands and congregate in thick masses on tidal mud flats and marshes. Considering the hunting practices at the time and the habits of the dowitchers, slaughter of these birds was inevitable. Gunners, including the Veritys, had market demands and, no doubt, thought there was an endless supply for their guns. This rare dowitcher is in full spring plumage and is in a graceful, pleasing attitude. The implication of spring plumage is profound in that the bird was hunted throughout the year without any respite from a daily barrage. In 1903 legislation was enacted to curtail spring shooting and in 1918, all shooting of migratory shorebirds was made illegal.

Collection of Russ J. and Karen Goldberger

Ruddy Duck

by Lee Dudley (1860-1942), Knotts Island, North Carolina

Fortunately Joel Barber, known affectionately as the "Father" of decoy collectors, made forays into most of the gunning areas of the East Coast. His research proved very important relative to the Dudley family history. In recent times, Richard McIntyre, collector and historian of Carolina decoys, completed the research of this famous maker. Joel Barber, author of *Wildfowl Decoys*, visited the Dudley farm in 1920. He actually interviewed Lee who by then was 60 years old. While there, Barber found a shed full of Lee's ruddy duck decoys. Dudley attested to the fact that he carved them during the 1890s when "the price of a ruddy duck soared to a dollar apiece." Dudley was part of a family of baymen and market gunners. All were involved in running gun clubs along the Carolina coast. This particular ruddy duck is branded "L.D." and is one of the decoys found by Barber. It has strong lines, and V-shaped carving in the tail which dates it to the 1890s. Because of the demand for big rigs of decoys, Dudley probably made hundreds. However, many were lost in storms, fires or simply used for firewood. Finding one in original paint is a rarity.

Private Collection

Canada Goose

by Charles Walker (1876-1954), Princeton, Illinois

G.B. Gibbs, a sportsman and lumberyard owner in Princeton, had the good fortune of knowing Charles Walker. Their chance meeting was predicated by Gibbs becoming a member of the Princeton Fish and Gun Club in 1919. Walker, who carved for members, was commissioned by Gibbs to carve a rig of six Canada geese. According to historians, this was the only rig of geese Walker ever made. Mr. Gibbs was a member of the Club into the 1940s, at which time the geese became available to collectors. The decoy pictured is hollow, with a removable head, is in original paint and branded "Gibbs" on the bottom. It is considered to be the finest and rarest of all Walker decoys. Further information on Walker can be found in *Decoy Magazine*, November 1992.

Collection of Joseph and Donna Tonelli

Canvasback Hen

by Albert D. Laing (1811-1886), New York City and Stratford, Connecticut

It is with good fortune that decoy historians, specifically Ronald S. Swanson in this case, took the time to research the life of Albert Laing. A wealth of knowledge has resulted. The reader may refer to "Decoy Magazine," July 1995 for a thorough and edifying article by Swanson. Laing was the son of a wealthy Quaker, a New York City merchant. He could afford to travel and in 1838 spent four months throughout France. Laing kept a diary of his trip and was inclined to chronicle his life, including his decoy hunting experiences. Most of Laing's carvings were done in the early to mid 1800s. He was a market gunner and sold his wares to the Fulton Fish Market in New York City. Much of Laing's gunning occurred near the city on Long Island Sound. He was one of the originators of the "Battery," a boat that sat flush with the water, surrounded by decoys including "wing ducks," laid on sideboards extending from the boat. Laing is further said to have taken his decoys and hunting prowess, including the use of the "Battery," to the Chesapeake Bay and Delaware River area. Hence, some of his decoys have been found in these locations. Pictured here is an early period wing duck canvasback. It is hollow and has a bottom board. Its aesthetically positioned head is carved to seduce the wary canvasback drake. Also pictured is Laing's original bound diary of hunting kills along with specific dates and species shot. Note the date: October, 1835.

Collection of Ronald S. Swanson

Canada Goose

by George (1830-1905) and James (1831-1884) Warin, Toronto, Canada

The Warins immigrated to Canada from England in 1832 and settled on the Toronto Peninsula. There, employed by their brother-in-law, they learned the skills of boat building and in 1873 established George and James Warin Boat Builders. The Warins quickly became famous craftsmen, making high quality rowing sculls and eventually sponsoring Ned Hanlan, who became the world single-handed rowing champion. The talents developed from making boats became the basis for their decoys; delicate, hollow, with graceful lines and stamped "G and J Warin, Makers, Toronto." In 1874, along with David Ward of Toronto, George Warin founded the St. Clair Flats Shooting Company in southwestern Ontario. There, his decoys became the focus of early Canadian collectors and continue to be highly prized today. During his lifetime, George was the most prominent sportsman in all of Canada. The Canada goose pictured exemplifies the graceful and delicate beauty of his work.

Collection of Russ J. and Karen Goldberger

Brant

by Nathan Cobb Jr. (1825-1905), Cobb Island, Virginia

This brant decoy, with its alert pose, is considered by many as the finest Cobb brant known. In 1994 it was the most expensive decoy sold in that year. Although there are a number of brants, few can equal this original-paint lure. Cobb expressed his artistic creativity and spatial concepts with each of his carvings. Temporally, it was a short period i.e., 1865 to 1890, that the Cobbs made decoys. A horrendous hurricane in 1893 struck Cobb Island and destroyed the Cobb Island Resort Hotel and outbuildings that were part of the Cobb enclave. This was a devastating loss!

Imagine also how many Cobb decoys were washed out to sea (incidentally, one is still occasionally found mired in a Northhampton County marsh or mud flat). Life changed on Cobb Island and although the sons of Nathan Sr. tried to revive the guiding and hunting enterprise, little came of it. Most all of the Cobb decoys are attributed to a period prior to '93. The multitudes of waterfowl must have welcomed the respite from the Cobb guns.

Collection of Lloyd Griffith, M.D.

Pintail Drake

by Charles Walker (1876-1954), Princeton, Illinois

The viewer should dwell on this elegant and beautifully sculptured decoy as it sits on the shores of Long Island Sound. Carved in 1930, it is one of two survivors of the rig of M. Brown. Walker made a rig of these pintails for Merle Brown who owned "Share #28" in the Princeton Game and Fish Club, an exclusive gunning club which sold a "share" to any new member. With it came decoys, a boat and so forth. This decoy still retains its "28" brand. Charles Walker was a house painter by trade. His decoy carving was a sideline, but became more important, although not prolific, as his fame grew. He eventually became the primary decoy carver for the Princeton Club and was in great demand both as a carver and guide. Many carvers and hunters would bring decoys to Walker to either paint or repaint. Therefore, an original Walker carving is rare and highly valued.

Collection of Alan and Elaine Haid

Mallard Drake

by Nicole Vidacovich Sr. (1853-1945), New Orleans, Louisiana

Known as "Mr. Derby" for his ever-present chapeau, Nicole grew up at the confluence of the Mississippi River and the Gulf of Mexico. Sportsmen from throughout the United States came to this area to hunt the waterfowl that congregated there each winter. Vidacovich became widely known as a consummate carver who produced a high-caliber decoy. His works included canvasbacks, pintails, ringnecks, coots, as well as mallards. This talent led Nicole to secure a job guiding at one of the most exclusive hunting clubs in the region — the Delta Duck Club.

The area encompassed by this turn-of-the-century enclave was purchased in 1937 by the Federal Government to create the 48,000-acre Delta National Wildlife Refuge. This mallard drake was made by Vidacovich during the late 1800s as a present for his wife. It is said to have traveled with him until his death in 1945. This rare decoy is considered the most classic and valuable of all Louisiana carvings.

Collection of Brian and Emilie Cheramie

Sickle-billed Curlew

by an unknown maker, Cape Cod, Massachusetts, circa 1890

On a rainy 1987 afternoon near Kittery, Maine, a racy sickle-billed curlew sold for $35,550. This was a significant sum for a shorebird by an unknown maker. Granted, Dr. John Phillips, a noted Massachusetts sportsman had only the best and this decoy was part of his collection. He was a friend of the legendary Elmer Crowell who made great decoys for Phillips. However, Crowell's name could not be identified with this decoy. The paint patterns and form are not Crowell's. It would have been intriguing to speculate how much the curlew would have sold for if we could name its maker. Move ahead to 1997. Great excitement was generated in Ogunquit, Maine, at the Guyette-Schmidt auction. The curlew had resurfaced and was touted by the auction house to now be worth $40,000 to $60,000. Rumor had it going possibly as high as $100,000. However, when the gavel fell, a new world record was established; $335,000, eclipsing an eleven-year record of $319,000 for an Elmer Crowell decorative preening pintail. Decoy investors take note!

Private Collection

Hissing Goose

by Nathan Cobb Jr. (1825-1905), Cobb Island, Virginia

This reaching or hissing hollow goose by Nathan Cobb Jr., circa 1880, was described as "exceedingly rare" when it was auctioned in 1993. Hence, a world record price was set for a Cobb decoy. Without question this is one of the finest Cobb geese known and is referred to by the collector as his "Marilyn Monroe!" It is pictured on page 123 in *Art Of The Decoy* by Adele Earnest, and was part of her collection. It can also be seen in *Southern Decoys* by Henry Fleckenstein, and *Decoys, A North American Survey*, by Gene and Linda Kangas. Despite the daily demands of helping to run Cobb Island Resort, Nathan Jr. was able to reflect on his decoy sculptures; making them not merely utilitarian, but artistically innovative. I am sure that his decoys, even then, were considered objects of beauty. This goose is not only a floater but was also used as a field or marsh stick-up.

Collection of Lloyd Griffith, M.D.

Wood Duck Drake

by Joseph Lincoln (1859-1938), Accord, Massachusetts

The wood duck drake is probably the most beautiful of all wild ducks. Its brilliant plumage and iridescent blue-green crest set it apart from all other waterfowl. The carver has a special obligation to fulfill a mandate that nature requires; authentic replication of the wood duck's beauty. Joe Lincoln succeeded! This decoy was part of the George Starr collection. Dr. Starr, a very prominent Massachusetts collector, considered this decoy to be his finest. After his death, Starr's collection was auctioned and the top bidder must have also concurred. It set a new world record at the time, $205,000. The story doesn't end here. The author photographed it at the original purchaser's home in Virginia. Several months later, while photographing a Minnesota collection, there sat the wood duck as the quintessential highlight of its new owner's display. According to its new owner, acquiring this special Lincoln wood duck was worth all the effort and money he expended. A thing of beauty is a joy forever.

Collection of James and Diane Cook

Merganser Hen

by George Boyd (1873-1941), Seabrook, New Hampshire

This fine decoy is probably the best example known of a solid-body decoy by Boyd. Most are canvas, covered over a molded wood frame with a wooden head and breast. Rarely did he make a solid-body lure. There is no question that Boyd was a very skilled craftsman. He made not only working decoys, but miniatures as well and it is said that he made more than seven hundred. Many were sold through Iver Johnson, a sporting goods store in Boston, Abercrombie and Fitch, and Macy's in New York City. His primary occupation was that of a shoemaker. In his workshop behind his house, he worked in his shoe repair business and found time to construct his decoys. Old cedar telephone poles and railroad ties provided the seasoned wood he needed. The condition of this merganser attests to the careful scrutiny that Boyd employed when choosing his wood and applying paint.

Collection of James McCleery, M.D.
*Private California Collection

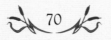

Shorebird Rig

by Harry V. Shourds Sr. (1861-1920), Tuckerton, New Jersey

This grouping of decoys, circa 1912, represents the finest shorebirds ever carved by Shourds. It was the intent of the author to photograph only the Ruddy Turnstone for this book. Pictured at the right is the only one known in this condition and is appraised for close to $80,000. However, these special "fat body" decoys are so unique as a group, they must all be shown. James Allen, noted New Jersey collector, stated "You think you've seen it all! Not true! These decoys are really unbelievable!" Pictured from left to right are a yellowlegs, knot, black-bellied plover, peep, fall plumage plover, dowitcher, curlew, immature black-bellied plover and the turnstone. Shourds' shorebirds are carved ordinarily in a flatter style and can be bought at most decoy auctions. This rig was carved after a request by Ash Millner, of Locustville, Virginia. Millner bought six to eight dozen shorebirds from Shourds. Millner was an oyster buyer and knew of Shourds through purchasing oysters dredged in Tuckerton. It is apparent that Shourds was truly a commercial carver and sold thousands of decoys during his productive years.

Collection of Cameron and Jean Troilo

Merganser Drake

by Cassius Smith (1847-1907), Milford, Connecticut

This beautiful red-breasted merganser was made in the mid 1880s and was no doubt part of a rig of decoys used by Smith, a noted market gunner and carver. Cassius' brother, George, owned a hotel in Milford and Cassius would supply waterfowl for its tables. The "Milford School" is characterized by a decoy that is hollow, has a flat top, rounded sides and is tapered toward a narrow breast. Shortly after World War II, D.A. Young of Mattituck, Long Island, found a rig of decoys attributed to Cassius Smith and later displayed in a private museum in Mattituck. The merganser pictured, is one of those decoys and still retains the "Young" brand and museum number.

Collection of Alan and Elaine Haid

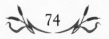

Snow Goose

by John Tax (1894-1967), Osakis, Minnesota

John Tax, known as the "Last of the Prairie Carvers," worked in his father's shoe repair and harness shop in Osakis. In 1928, he took over the business and also began to carve decoys. He made a unique canvas-covered lure which was very functional, although not aesthetically appealing. He later used basswood, pine and cedar boards laminated together to form blocks. From these he fashioned magnificent standing Canada geese, snow geese, mallards and floating decoys. Most of his patterns were after Audubon and Tax's paint exemplifies this direction. Tax is also noted for his fine ice spearing fish decoys which he stamped "John Tax, Osakis, Minnesota." This feeding snow goose is of laminated construction and, according to the collector, is the only one known in original paint.

Collection of James and Patricia Doherty

Pair of Whimbrels

by William Bowman (1824-1906), Old Town, Maine

These two Bowman decoys are referred to in the *Audubon Society Field Guide To North American Birds*, as whimbrels or Hudsonian curlews. This particular marsh bird is the size of a crow and very wary in its nesting habits. Massive flocks migrate down the coast to South America in the fall and return each spring to the Arctic Tundra via the mid-North American flyway. Eskimo curlews were virtually extinct when Bowman made his summer excursions to Lawrence, Long Island, to shoot shorebirds. Hence, we have only found Hudsonians, dowitchers, plovers, yellowlegs, long-billed curlews and ruddy turnstone decoys made by Bowman. All these species were plentiful and ready for Bowman's gun. Bowman certainly captured the aesthetic essence of the species he carved. Detail was given to body musculature and wing conformation. His paint was applied with a masterly hand. These two curlews, a high-head and a low-head, were part of the Nina Fletcher Little collection. Both were sold in 1994 at Sothebys, New York City and the low-head brought a record price of $90,500.

Private Collection

Canada Goose and Pintail Drake

by Elmer Crowell (1862-1952), East Harwich, Massachusetts

These two fine decoys characterize different significant periods of Crowell's carvings. The Canada goose is referred to as a pre-stamped decoy and was carved between 1890 and 1915; probably closer to 1900. It has an elongated body form, which is unique for a Crowell goose. Note the pulled back and tucked head position. It was sold at Skinner's Auction Gallery in Bolton, Massachusetts, and brought a significant sum for an early pre-stamped decoy. This turned-head pintail, which measures twenty inches end-to-end and was carved circa 1916, has Crowell's oval stamp stating "A. Elmer Crowell Decoys, Harwich, Mass." Most collectors consider decoys with the oval stamp to be Crowell's finest work. Interestingly, this decoy, which was never used, is inscribed in pencil under the bill by Crowell, "Brooks $5.00." He had made it for Chester R. Brooks (1866-1963) of Cleveland, Ohio. Brooks owned an extensive waterfowl preserve on Lake Erie, close to Cleveland. He was a member of Winous Point and Cedar Point Gun Clubs, near Sandusky, Ohio. His relationship with Elmer Crowell is unanswered and certainly will remain a mystery.

Crowell Goose-Collection of John and Lois Horgan
Crowell Pintail-Private Collection

Curlew Decoy

by an unknown maker, circa 1890-1900, Cape Cod, Massachusetts

This curlew is photographed far-removed from Cape Cod; in the background is the Pacific Ocean. Nevertheless, any setting for this wonderful piece of New England folk art is adequate. A Cambridge, Massachusetts auctioneer had gone to the Thousand Islands, New York to appraise an estate and incidentally found one of the best split-tail Cape Cod curlews ever seen. At auction, it brought the year's (1997) eleventh highest price for a decoy. Note the delicate lines of the two-piece construction and the graceful neck and head carving. The ability of this decoy to survive one hundred years, considering its fragile construction, is remarkable. Cape Cod was a natural stopover for migrating shorebirds and no doubt, many were shot over this fine lure.

Private California Collection

Mallard Drake

by the Caines Brothers, Georgetown, South Carolina, circa 1890-1900

The Caines brothers, Hucks, Ball, Sawney and Bob, like many of their contemporaries in the late 1800s were active market gunners. They supplied fresh waterfowl to satisfy the palates of Charleston, Greenville and Raleigh. But more importantly they carved decoys! What set them apart from their peers, however, was the uniqueness of their style. Their rigs were made of cypress and tupelo gum (both native to the area) and are either hollow or solid body. Even though the Caines were exposed to the decoys sportsmen and market gunners brought to the area from the North, no other carver of North America had any influence on their creativity. The preening mallard drake shown here came from the William Yawkey estate on South Island. Situated at the mouth of Winyah Bay in Georgetown County, this island was purchased in 1911 from General Eliot Porter Alexander, a Confederate general, by Yawkey who at the time was a wealthy financier and owner of the Detroit Tigers. In 1914, William died and his 16-year-old nephew, Tom, inherited both the Islands and the Tigers. Tom went on to also own the Boston Red Sox. In 1991, Tom's widow, Jean, died and this decoy was sold at auction for $165,000.

Courtesy of "Collectible Old Decoys"

Herring Gull

by Harry V. Shourds Sr. (1861-1920), Tuckerton, New Jersey

This is one of two gull floaters that are known to survive to this date. Shourds may have carved more but they did not survive the rigors of daily abuse by the hunters. Most ducks and seagulls are not compatible since gulls will kill crippled ducks and their chicks. Therefore the use of herons or gulls as confidence decoys had to be selective. Both the colors of the gull and its size lent itself to be used more in brant rigs. Brant, or geese, are not threatened by gulls and because gulls are very wary, the sight of several in a rig would add to the magnetism of the stools. Between Tuckerton and the outer sandbars are the Sea Dog Shoals; sand bars created by the tidal run from the ocean inlet into the Barnegat Bay. It was the primary gunning area for sink-box hunters to shoot both geese and brant, and no doubt, this decoy was used at that site to add a different dimension to the gunning rig. Many consider that the gull pictured here is one of Shourds' finest decoys.

Collection of James McCleery, M.D.
* Collection of James and Patricia Doherty

Canada Goose

by Henry Kilpatrick (1868-1935), Barnegat, New Jersey

This Canada goose typifies the upper Barnegat Bay style or school of carving. Kilpatrick was a contemporary of Henry Grant and Cooper Predmore, both Barnegat residents and noted Bay Area carvers. Kilpatrick lures are characterized by a high, full tail with a suggestion of a wing-tip carving or hump near the tail. They also have the traditional or pinched face through the eye line. Kilpatrick, like so many of his peers, was a market gunner and carver for the trade. A large rig of unused, circa 1910, geese and brant, including this goose, was found in a Philadelphia coal bin. They were all wrapped in paper and apparently stored for more than sixty years. This goose retains some of the paper, which has adhered to its side. It is also the exact decoy, plate 234, in *New Jersey Decoys*, Henry Fleckenstein.

Collection of Peter Bartlett

Wood Duck Drakes, Premier Grade

by the Mason Company (1890-1918), Detroit, Michigan

The reader should pay special attention to these circa 1908-1912 Mason decoys. In April 1998, the collector bought the Mason on the left for $350,000; setting a new world record for any decoy. This wood duck, which is the only one known, has been the envy of every collector and has been coveted by all who have seen it. The William Mackey collection sold in the early 1970s but the family held onto several decoys, including this one. Finally, offers led to negotiation and hence its sale. The Mason Company was the premier producer of decoys at the turn of the century. Three models were made, the Standard or Detroit model, the Challenge grade and the most elaborate and expensive, the Premier grade. All species were made including the ruddy duck which, incidentally, has never been found.

This Premier grade wood duck is truly top-of-the-line in form and paint. It is accompanied by a rare Premier grade salesman sample. Lack of this species at the turn of the century created little demand for wood duck decoys. Hence, few were ordered or carved by gunners, making any survivors rare and very expensive. As part of the McCleery collection they were auctioned in January 2000 and sold for, left to right, $356,000 and $24,000. Both decoys are pictured in *Mason Decoys*, by Russ Goldberger and Alan Haid, 1993.

Collection of James McCleery, M.D.
*Collection of Ronald Gard
*Collection of James and Dailene Goodman

Green-winged Teals

by Elmer Crowell (1862-1952), East Harwich, Massachusetts

These teals are another example of the artistry of Elmer Crowell. Carved circa 1915 for the rig of Dr. John Phillips, they exemplify the period when Crowell began using his oval brand. The brands are characterized by a "hard ring" which dates them to the 1915 period. This was when Crowell was at his best. Both birds have carved primaries and carved tails. The drake is pictured on page 107 in *New England Decoys* by John Delph. Without question, these are the best pair of Crowell green-winged teals known. Commercially, Crowell made mostly black ducks, pintails, redheads, scaup, goldeneyes, geese and brants. These species were the primary targets for the market gunners. Crowell admitted that he was disappointed with the 1918 laws that limited shooting of migratory waterfowl. He was quoted as saying, "Those were the days for me. Now the fun has gone out of it." After this date, Crowell's production of decoys dropped dramatically.

Collection of Alan and Elaine Haid

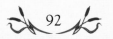

Pintails

by Dave "Umbrella" Watson (1851-1938), Chincoteague, Virginia

Watson was an early settler of Chincoteague Island. In his heyday the island was a natural harvest site for migratory waterfowl. Watson, who got his nickname from the habit of always carrying an umbrella, was a talented decoy carver and was naturally attracted to the opportunity to make a living "off the water." He guided, supplied decoys to hunters and sold his lures to various gun clubs. One such club in North Carolina, the Gooseville Gun Club, ordered pintails and black ducks from Watson. Some of his decoys are found with the brand "Gooseville Gun Club" on the bottom. All his lures have glass eyes and a distinctive brow line, giving the birds a look of hostility. They also have a distinctly carved tail and a very subtle raised wing "V" carving. Because coastal decoys were primarily used in salt water, many were frequently repainted. These pintails, carved circa 1910, were spared that fate. Despite living and working in a small community throughout his life, little information has been found regarding Watson's personal history. We can conclude, however, that he made a fine decoy typical of the Virginia Eastern Shore.

Collection of William and Kaye Purnell

Canada Goose

by Nathan Cobb Jr. (1825-1905), Cobb Island, Virginia

The story of the Cobb family is a romance! James Michner could have fashioned a book titled *The Eastern Shore*, and made the Cobb family its driving force. Nathan Cobb Sr. was born in Eastham, Massachusetts, in 1797 and was a descendent of Stephen Hopkins Jr., who came to Plymouth on the Mayflower. Nathan and his wife, Nancy, had three sons, Nathan Jr. in 1825, Warren in 1833 and Albert in 1836. Because of Nancy's poor health the family moved south and landed in Northhampton County, Virginia. In 1839, the family purchased Sand Shoal Island, situated eight miles from the mainland, which later became known as Cobb Island. There, the family prospered, built a hotel and offered fine accommodations, dining, bathing and, of course, great waterfowl hunting. Guiding sportsmen and market gunning were both important for the Cobbs. This necessitated what today is considered the greatest of all waterfowl folk art: the Cobb Family geese, shorebirds and duck decoys. This wonderful reaching-head goose was in the American Bird Sculpture exhibit at the Smithsonian Institute in 1987 and is so labeled. It has the Mackey stamp and William Purnell brand. It was photographed beside the Ward Museum of Wildfowl Art, Salisbury, Maryland, where it was on display.

Private California Collection

Black-bellied Plover

by Elmer Crowell (1862-1952), East Hardwich, Massachusetts

The three "Dust Jacket" Black-bellied Plovers by Crowell are his most famous shorebird carvings. These decoys adorn the cover of *American Bird Decoys*, by William Mackey Jr. To own one of these lures is to have a significant share of decoying history. After Joel Barber, the "Father of Decoy Collectors," Mackey is the most important name in decoy collecting. He was an avid historian and his research led to much knowledge of the great carvers and their work. Mackey considered this particular plover to be one of Elmer Crowell's greatest accomplishments. Crowell captured the true essence of a live shorebird in motion. Mackey noted "...the scattering of shot holes is proof of their baptism by fire." The form, raised and carved wing carvings, dates this decoy to the early 1900s.

Collection of Theodore and Judith Harmon

Swan

by an unknown maker, St. Clair Flats, Mitchell Bay, Canada, circa 1880

This elegant and graceful swan decoy is one of six originally made by an unknown Toronto carver. They eventually became part of the hunting rig of the St. Clair Flats Shooting Company; an exclusive gunning club on Lake St. Clair. It is evident that swans were actively gunned during this period as opposed to their present use as confidence decoys. This particular decoy is very hollow with a thin bottom board. It is branded F. H. Walker, a member of the Club from 1890-1914. It is the only one to survive in original paint and the influence of the "Toronto School," is apparent, that is, delicate light-weight decoys, hollow with bottom boards secured at the perimeter by fine nails. Photographs of this decoy appear in many publications and articles including *The Great Book Of Wildfowl Decoys*, by Joe Engers. The present owners have employed this decoy as the logo for their decoy advertising.

Collection of Alan and Elaine Haid

Merganser Drake

by Captain Charles G. Osgood (1820-1886), Salem, Massachusetts

Historians Ronald Swanson and Jackson Parker have uncovered the legend of Charles Osgood. Through intensive detective work it has been determined that Osgood was an active decoy carver and hunter in the Rowley River Basin near Salem, Massachusetts. He was employed as a sea captain and worked for Francis Peabody Esq. of Salem. Osgood made voyages in the Calcutta, Bombay and Canton trades. While on these lengthy trips, it is purported that he carved his decoys, including a rig of geese, mergansers and other species. The mergansers, which number no more than eight, are both solid and hollow. Upswept tails and bottom boards mark the hollow variety; all are superbly carved and painted. Osgood died suddenly of a heart attack in 1886. The merganser pictured sold in the high five figures in a 1994 auction. Its rarity is apparent.

Collection of Richard and Vereen Coen

Pintail Drake Ice Duck

by Charles Schoenheider Sr. (1856-1944), Peoria, Illinois

According to one collector and reviewer for this book, this pintail represents the "icon" of Illinois River decoys. Few areas of North America have flocks of migratory pintails as consistent and in as great numbers as the Central Flyway. Mallards, black ducks, teals and wood ducks are pandemic; not pintails. When we review auction catalogs and the noted decoy collections, nine out of ten pintails were carved by Ontario and Mississippi Flyway makers. Schoenheider, a market gunner who traveled the Illinois River south of Peoria, was no exception. He carved many pintails, mallards and teals. In later life, he carved floating and standing geese decoys. The pictured pintail is hollow, of pine and cedar construction and probably painted by his long-time friend and hunting companion, Jack Franks. Franks, a professional painter and decorator, gave the birds a detailed feather pattern and used a graining comb to complete the surface. This decoy is one of several that were on display at the G.N. Portman Sporting Goods Co. in Peoria. When the store closed in 1925, the decoys were taken to the East Coast where this decoy and a fine mallard ice duck were auctioned.

Collection of James and Diane Cook

Canada Goose

by George Boyd (1873-1941), Seabrook, New Hampshire

George Boyd was virtually unheard of as a decoy maker until the early 1970s. His masterfully carved and painted shorebirds were a mystery unsolved until research revealed their maker. Boyd was an early market gunner like so many of his decoy-carving contemporaries. The marshes of Seabrook afforded him the opportunity to observe all forms of waterfowl. Boyd developed his own distinctive form of carving; since he was not in the vicinity of any other noted carvers, only his own interpretation prevailed.

His easily distinguished shorebirds have squared off heads, known as "beetles," complimented by short brush strokes. Geese, black ducks and mergansers also have beautiful flowing lines. Many of his decoys are made with canvas stretched over a wooden frame. They also have a carved head and breast of pine construction. This reaching Canada goose is rare and exceptionally sculptured. It represents Boyd at his finest.

Private Collection

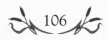

American Merganser Drake

by an unknown maker, Cape Cod, Massachusetts, circa 1910

Although saltwater marshes and tidal flats surround Cape Cod, there are a significant number of freshwater ponds. The American (or Common Merganser) is much more likely to frequent the latter sites. When ponds ice over, the mergansers move to rivers where they are usually seen in large flocks, facing upstream and diving in unison for prey. This decoy, with its elegant paint and form, is part of a pair that was gunned over in the early part of the 20th century. There is no history of market gunners shooting American Mergansers, but this fact doesn't preclude the possibility. It is probable that this decoy was more of an expression by an unknown carver to exercise his artistic skills. Finding an American Merganser by an East Coast carver is extremely rare. This decoy, along with its mate, is pictured in *Top Of The Line Collectibles*, by Donna Tonelli, p. 91 and *New England Decoys*, by John and Shirley Delph, p. 71 (note the curious visitor to this floating decoy).

Collection of James and Diane Cook

Widgeon Drake Preener

by Elmer Crowell (1862-1952), East Harwich, Massachusetts

Decoys carved by Elmer Crowell reach a plateau not achieved by other carvers. This preener carved circa 1900, was made as a working lure for Dr. John Phillips, Crowell's employer. Phillips hired Crowell as his gunning camp manager, guide and decoy maker. It is difficult to imagine that Crowell would make a rig of these beautiful widgeons to gun over. No doubt, it was a special gift to Dr. Phillips and was ultimately a part of his estate. It certainly qualifies as being in the top one hundred decoys of North America, if not the top ten. Note the characteristic carving of this period; raised wing tips and rasping behind the head and on the breast illustrate Crowell at his best. Crowell also made many miniature shorebirds, songbirds and all other waterfowl species, as well as decorative carvings. In the Shelburne Museum, Shelburne, Vermont, there is a large and magnificent display of Crowell's work. It is housed in the Dorset House, which is specifically dedicated to premier decoy carvings.

Collection of James and Diane Cook

Rig of Merganser Decoys

by an unknown maker, Portland, Maine, circa 1910-1920

These very rare and unique decoys are described as shadow or silhouette in form. Their uniqueness is based on the fact that the necks and heads are carved in a three-dimensional fashion. Each has an oak bill that is inletted into the head and secured by a vertical dowel. Note how the preener's bill is integrated into the body. Mergansers were often sought by turn of the century gunners, especially along the Atlantic coast. There was no doubt, despite the merganser's fishy taste, a viable market for their kills. These decoys were part of a larger rig that were fastened to a floating board and anchored in front of the gunner's blind. Without question, this rig of decoys represents great American folk art and despite their frequent use in salt water, they retain their original paint. It would have been remiss of the author not to photograph them as an ensemble; they are also pictured in this arrangement on pages 108-109 of *New England Decoys*, John and Shirley Delph, published in 1981.

Collection of Loy and Rae Harrell

Green-winged Teal Drake

by Charles Perdew (1874-1963), Henry, Illinois

The owner of this exquisite Perdew carving has an affinity for collecting sleeper and preener decoys carved by famous Illinois River makers. This is a fine example of an early, circa 1915, decoy carved by Perdew and painted by his wife, Edna. Edna's paint is considered to be skillful and artistic. She had that responsibility from circa 1900 to the early 1940s when she became ill. Most of Perdew's early decoys had a V-shaped keel designed to float in fast-moving water. This pictured teal is an example of that style. It is the only known example of a Perdew teal drake sleeper. Teals are among the fastest-flying ducks and are hence, popular game birds.

Private California Collection

Canada Goose

by Joseph Lincoln (1859-1938), Accord, Massachusetts

By the turn of the 20th century, Joe Lincoln's reputation as a decoy carver was well established. He had been carving since he was a teenager; had advertised in local newspapers and disseminated his decoys throughout New England. Still carving at age 70, Lincoln had a drive unparalleled in decoying annals. His simple and unsophisticated style is best described as seductive. His lures personify what should be their utilitarian nature. Lincoln had use of native cedar and seasoned pine for construction. Unfortunately, many of his solid blocks, especially geese and brant, eventually developed a significant bottom split. This flaw is now considered a hallmark for a "good" Lincoln decoy. This hissing Canada goose sold in 1986 for $90,000. In 1926 it sold for $4. The 1986 price was a record at that time for a Lincoln decoy. It has now been surpassed by the sale of his wood duck drake for $300,000.

Private Collection

Canvasbacks

by John Graham (1822-1912), Charlestown, Maryland

John Graham was born in Charlestown in 1822, one of twelve children of Zachariah Graham. His grandfather, William, was listed as a resident of that village in the first census of the United States taken in 1790. The family tradition was cabinet making and undertaking. John followed in these footsteps. The ability to make fine furniture and the demands of duck hunting led to his carving of good functional decoys. Charlestown was also noted for other fine carvers such as William Heverin (1860-1951), George W. Barnes (1861-1915) and Wally Algard (1883-1959). Graham, however, is considered to be the originator of the Cecil County style decoy; that is, a paddle tail, a distinctive shelf on which the decoy's neck is attached, and often a "Roman nose." This pair of original-paint canvasbacks was made circa 1870 and is in structurally excellent condition. The profile illustrates the Cecil County style.

Private Collection

Pintail Drake

by Lem (1896-1984) and Steve (1895-1976) Ward, Chrisfield, Maryland

Not enough can be said about the ability and artistry of the Ward brothers. Their creative expression sculptured in decoys represents American folk art at its finest. This wonderful pintail was a favorite of Lem's and his special effort, as its painter, is evident. There was a profound evolution from the early 1920s to the 1930s in style and form. Most collectors prefer this latter period for the aesthetically pleasing attitude and painting of Ward decoys. This pintail drake represents all that is great during the 1930s era. Its high, Viking ship-like squared off head, long sweeping tail and bold vivid colors are special. On the bottom is painted a banner and signed atop, "Ward Decoys, Chrisfield, M.D." It also has two Mackey family stamps and is dated 1932. This is one of the decoys retained by the Mackey family, which also included the Mason premier wood duck. When this pintail came to auction in 1998 it established a new world record for a Ward decoy.

Collection of James and Diane Cook

Canada Goose

by Enoch Reindahl (1904-), Houghton, Wisconsin

As of this writing, Enoch Reindahl is still alive and well. Obviously he no longer carves decoys, but his recollections are vivid. In the late 1930s and 1940s he began making and selling his fine birds. He was so enamored by the beauty of waterfowl that he painstakingly carved and painted each decoy to simulate a live bird. In a 1949 *Sports Afield* article by Reindahl, titled "How to Make Decoys" he was not only instructive, but had several photographs of his working stools on the water. An example photograph is found on page 132 of *Top Of The Line Hunting Collectibles*, Donna Tonelli. This Canada goose has a detachable head, is hollow, has raised wing tips and is signed by Reindahl. Wisconsin is historically rich in carving and gunning tradition. Its many lakes and marshes make it a major flyway. As a result, carvers like Reindahl, Gus Moak, Warren Dettman, Owen Gromme, Ferd Homme, Joseph Seiger and Frank Strey, have become sought-after makers. An important reference is *Decoys Of The Winnebago Lakes*, Ronald Koch, 1988.

Collection of James and Diane Cook

Pintail Drake

by John Blair Sr. (1842-1928), Philadelphia, Pennsylvania

If you are someday asked what is the finest John Blair Sr. decoy, refer the questioner to the photograph at your right. This decoy fits all the criteria for an example of American folk art at its best. It is the classic form, hollow, sports a round bottom, high neck shelf and exquisite paint pattern. Somers Headley, a Delaware collector of many years, owned this decoy; it was the highlight of his collection. In 1994, it was auctioned in Easton, Maryland. The hammer fell at $132,000 — a record for a Blair decoy. This carving is considered the finest Delaware River decoy known. Can you picture a rig of these pintails in the fast-moving waters of the Delaware River? This sleek form, specifically designed for river gunning, had to be a source of pride for Blair as he watched flocks of pintails circle and drop into his rig. The pintail, because of its tasty flesh and fast flight, is a very popular North American game bird, especially in the West and Midwest.

Collection of James and Patricia Doherty

Canvasback Drake Preener

by Elmer A. Crowell (1862-1952), East Hardwich, Massachusetts

Cape Cod has a rich history of waterfowling. This was a natural stopover for migrating ducks, geese and shorebirds coming from nesting grounds in the Arctic. By the time Elmer Crowell was 14 years old, he was carving decoys and actively market gunning. This was to be his life. In 1898, at the age of 36, he became the guide and manager of a gunning camp owned by a wealthy physician, Dr. Phillips of Beverly, Massachusetts. This lasted for seven years, after which Crowell became a full-time carver. Decoys of this period do not have the Crowell stamp so familiar to most collectors. They have, in fact, carved primary feathers and carved crossed wing tips as seen in this photograph. Some collectors feel that decoys by Crowell from this early period are his best work and are the most valuable. The sculptured innovations and painting techniques by Crowell are unsurpassed and certainly epitomized by this rare and beautiful canvasback.

Private California Collection

Black Duck Sleeper

by Robert Elliston (1847-1915), Bureau, Illinois

This Elliston decoy, circa 1885, is the only black duck he made. It is also the only over-sized decoy Elliston carved. It is truly one-of-a-kind! When it was auctioned in 1984, it established a world record for an Illinois River carving: $16,500. A lot has happened since then. Its value now is in excess of $50,000! Elliston did not specifically carve decoys for his own use. He was a commercial maker and divided his time by caring for his family apiary in the summer and decoy carving in the winter. There was great demand for his lures and each evening he would whittle five or six heads and the next day would affix them to newly carved hollow bodies. A lead strip fastened to the bottom was stamped "The Elliston Decoy." Elliston was blessed by his partner and wife, Catherine, who painted all the decoys. Her paint was done in a stylized artistic manner that was to set the precedent for all future Illinois River carvers. Elliston was often visited by a young Charles Perdew, who went on to emulate his tutor. Catherine survived her husband and instructed other noted carvers on the art of painting decoys. A detailed history of the Elliston family may be found in an article by Donna Tonelli in *Decoy Magazine*, November 1991.

Collection of Alan and Elaine Haid

Merganser Hen

by John Dawson (1889-1959), Trenton, New Jersey

It would be remiss of the author not to include a Dawson-Dawson decoy in this publication. This refers to a decoy that is both carved and painted by Dawson. Much is made of John English decoys painted by Dawson. These particular decoys sell for high figures at auction. Dawson, however, carved a decoy that is certainly remote in style from most Delaware River decoys. They tend to be blocky, hollow with flat bottoms. Pictured is a fine merganser ice duck used in late winter on the Delaware River. Mergansers are the most sought after of Dawson's carvings. Dawson was a potter by trade but duck hunting was his true passion. He spent most of his spare time between 1905 and 1929, carving and gunning the Delaware River. He later became an active ecologist, engaged in the preservation of the Delaware River Waterway.

Collection of David and Jeanne Campbell

Mallard Hen

by Charles Perdew (1874-1963), Henry, Illinois

This mallard is considered one of the finest decoys ever carved by Perdew. It is a sleepy-eye style, with carved cheeks and raised wings. Perdew painted it circa 1940. It was given with a matching mallard to "Saccy" Saccaro of Spring Valley, Illinois and the Mud Lake Gun Club, as payment for getting saw blades for Perdew during World War II. In 1899, Perdew settled in Henry, Illinois and began his now famous career as a decoy carver, gunsmith and boat builder. He also made crow and duck calls, which were elaborately carved and decorated. Perdew patented his crow calls in 1909 and advertised his wares in national sporting and gunning magazines. Both he and his wife, Edna, painted Perdew's decoys. Her paint is considered more artistic than Henry's and most all of the carvings from 1899 to 1940 are adorned with Edna's touch. This decoy, however, is considered Perdew's finest paint and is a testament to his skill.

Collection of Joseph and Donna Tonelli

Eskimo Curlews

by the Folger Family, Nantucket, Massachusetts, circa 1850

This array of shorebirds represent the epitome of great Nantucket decoys. Nantucket has a rich history of shorebird shooting. It has always been a major stopover for migrating curlews, plovers, dowitchers, willets and certainly for most duck species. Whaling was also an important source of income and a major industry on the island. Baleen, a tough fibrous filtering system, available from a variety of whales including the blue and humpback, provided many carvers with strong, pliable, easily carved bills for their shorebirds. These six decoys, in fact, have baleen bills and are, remarkably, in excellent condition. Another issue relative to rarity is the eskimo curlew per se. Hunted unmercifully from its nesting grounds in Ungava Bay, through the Maritimes and down the East Coast, their numbers gradually decreased to the point that by 1890 they became virtually extinct. Of course the Folger family, market gunners on the Island, saw millions of these curlews, never realizing this majestic bird's ultimate fate.

Private Collection

Eider Drake

by an unknown maker, Maine Coast, circa 1920

Can you imagine a rig of these majestic eiders bobbing in the cold, uninviting waters of the rocky Maine coast? My inclination would be to rescue and quickly sequester them to a shelf in my home. Fortunately in 1990 this elegant eider was accidentally found by a Maine "picker" — one who looks in old barns, fishing shanties and boat houses for anything he or she can turn for a dollar. The beauty of this sculpture is unsurpassed; it has an inletted head, original stylized paint pattern and is structurally perfect. At auction, the "picker" had a significant reward for his effort. It is worth noting that eiders will easily and readily decoy into any makeshift rig. Therefore this decoy is an expression of a true artist. It was carved not just to lure the birds, but to satisfy the eye.

Collection of James McCleery, M.D.

Pintail Hen

by John English (1848-1915), Florence, New Jersey

Many of the top one hundred decoys originate from the 19th century. The reason is obvious! During the late part of that century until circa 1920, market gunning was an important source of income for many people. Carving decoys was a necessity, for few were available on a commercial basis. True craftsmen, such as English, were cabinetmakers, boat builders and basically people with a profound artistic capacity. Decoys by John English exemplify the art and beauty of this period. Fine, delicate, light hollow lures were his forté. Yet these objects of art were very functional. It is evident that English took pride in the structural beauty and the fine paint he applied to his decoys. This rare pintail hen is in original paint and structurally perfect. It's cylindrical body form was made to float realistically in the fast-moving waters of the Delaware River where it decoyed in the notoriously wary pintail. Charles Willey, a close friend and neighbor of English, supplied all the wood for the decoys. In exchange, English gave Willey several decoys including this pintail hen. Fortunately, Willey was not a hunter and the decoys sat on a shelf, accounting for the pristine condition of this beautiful John English creation.

Collection of Robert and Pauline White

Mallard Drake Ice Duck

by Charles Schoenheider Sr. (1856-1944), Peoria, Illinois

This graceful and lifelike decoy adorned the shelves of Portman's Gun Store in Peoria, Illinois from circa 1900 to 1925. Charles L. Portman was well known to most of the famous Illinois Rivers carvers, including Schoenheider, Robert Elliston, Bert Graves, Charles Purdew and Hiram Hotze. He was proprietor of the Peoria Arms Company from 1900 to 1925 and his business attracted gunners and carvers alike. Schoenheider placed several of his ice ducks, including this standing mallard, in Portman's store as advertisement for his commercial decoy business. These were ingenuous lures, made to stand on icy marsh edges or on a submerged log near the blind. It is easy to picture a flock of wary mallards pitching to a rig of Schoendeider decoys. This particular mallard was chosen to grace the cover of *The Great Book Of Wildfowl Decoys*, by Joe Engers.

Collection of James and Diane Cook

Mallard Hen

by Nathan R. Horner, (1881-1942), West Creek, New Jersey

Rowley Horner was a true master of his art. It is plausible that whatever endeavor he undertook, he was more than successful. Besides carving decoys and guiding "Sports," Horner was a boat builder, sail maker and an accomplished musician. Whether he was the master of these latter talents we can only speculate. We do know about his decoy carving. Basically a pupil of Harry V. Shourds, Horner learned well. Along with his uncle, Ellis Parker, and friend, Chris Sprague, many smoothly refined hollow lures were created. This mallard hen is the epitome of his finest effort. James Allen of Tuckerton, New Jersey, told the author: "This is the best painted decoy in existence. Its wet on wet paint technique has created a Horner masterpiece." This decoy was part of the John Hillman collection and when auctioned in 1996 it brought $82,500, a record for a Horner lure.

Collection of Richard and Vereen Coen

Curlew

by Thomas Gelston (1851-1924), Brooklyn and Quogue, New York

Gelston was the son of a well-to-do sportsman and land developer in Brooklyn, New York. This was close to the Sheepshead Bay marshes where Gelston first experienced shorebird hunting. His family spent summers at Quogue, Long Island on Shinnecock Bay. It was here that Gelston settled in as a "gentleman hunter." The term implying that he spent more time carving decoys or hunting than he did working. Many of his duck carvings were constructed of cork or wood and sometimes both. These lures were not as aesthetically pleasing as his shorebirds. Here he became the true artist! His curlews are Gelston's greatest contribution to the folk art history of Long Island. This decoy, circa 1900, is in the running position and is in outstanding original paint.

Collection of Lloyd Griffith, M.D.

144

Canvasback Hen

by Charles "Shang" Wheeler (1872-1949), Stratford, Connecticut

Who says politics and decoy carving don't mix? Wheeler, a three-term politician was asked to run for governor of Connecticut by a group of his political allies. His response was: "A governor should be married — I'm not married. A governor should attend church — I like to fish on Sundays!" This was typical independent Shang. However, while in political office in the 1920s he was instrumental in enacting legislation to control pollution in Connecticut waterways and to control land development. His spare time was spent in his workshop and on the water. Wheeler found time to carve spectacular decoys and won many best-in-show ribbons for his effort. Wheeler also made decorative fish, assorted waterfowl and songbird carvings. This particular canvasback sleeper was part of Wheeler's estate and was later in the collection of Tom Marshall, one of Wheeler's close friends. Dixon Merkt pictures it on page 145 in his book, *Shang*. It is more than interesting to note that in 1949, when Wheeler died, his attorney offered to sell seventy-five Wheeler decoys for $1,000. He couldn't find a buyer!

Collection of Alan and Elaine Haid

Black Brant

by George William McLellan (1897-1987), Eureka, California

On the rugged upper coast of California, just south of the Oregon line, lies Humbolt Bay. This large water mass is traditionally a stopover for migrating West Coast waterfowl. McLellan, a life-long resident of Eureka and plumber for fifty years, was a talented decoy carver. He made large rigs of floaters, including very stylized black brants. However, his rig of nine brant flyers is his true contribution to waterfowl art. They were made in the late 1930s and were constructed from a redwood log. Each was suspended at varying levels on telescoping rods; the wind created a wavering movement that simulated flight. The wings are spruce frames over which is laid stiff butcher paper and then muslin. They fit into the body with locking clips and are hinged to create motion. McLellan decoys rank at the top of the 20th century carving tradition of the West Coast. A photograph of McLellan and detailed sketches of his flyers can be found in *Wildfowl Decoys Of The West Coast*, Michael Miller and Frederick Hanson.

Collection of David and Andrea Fischer

Canada Goose

by Captain Charles G. Osgood (1820-1886), Salem, Massachusetts

Framed by the Dorset House, Shelburne Museum, Shelburne, Vermont, an Osgood goose sits perched, preening its feathers. What a magnificent and beautifully sculptured decoy! Osgood must have been heavenly inspired when he made his famous rig of geese. All are now housed in the Shelburne Museum. A letter from George G. Frelinghuysen to the author states, "I bought the Canadian geese years ago from 'John and Henry,' dealers for my shop on Park Avenue. A Mrs. Divine from New Jersey bought them but returned saying they would not float in her swimming pool. My mother, Mrs. P.H.B. Frelinghuysen, gave them to her sister, Mrs. J. W. Webb, for the Shelburne Museum."

Captain Osgood, a Salem, Massachusetts sea captain, made worldwide voyages and carved this rig of decoys while at sea. They are hollow with bottom boards and have removable heads, which are uniquely fastened to its respective neck shelf. Each component has a Roman numeral, which matches its companion piece. This particular decoy is the epitome of folk art and without question is considered North America's most valuable.

Collection of Shelburne Museum, Shelburne, Vermont

Buffleheads

by Nathan Rowley Horner (1861-1940), West Creek, New Jersey

When one carver creates decoys that warrant exposure to the public, it behooves the author to do exactly that. Besides Horner's wonderful widgeons and mallards, this pair of buffleheads qualify in the ranks of Horner's top decoys. The fast-flying and elusive bufflehead is diminutive in size and difficult to shoot. Hence it would have been rare for a market gunner to order them. It has to be assumed that Horner made these decoys to satisfy his own creative energy or as a special order for someone.

Their rarity is obvious. These decoys were owned by Somers Headley, a noted Delaware collector, and it is purported that he obtained them in the 1950s directly from the Horner family. In 1994 they were auctioned for $71,000. This photograph was taken on a hot and steamy Texas morning.

Collection of James McCleery, M.D.
*Collection of Cameron and Jean Troilo

Brant

by Chauncey "Chance" Wheeler (1862-1937), Alexandria Bay, New York

Situated near the juncture of the St. Lawrence River and Lake Ontario, Alexandria Bay became a Mecca for East Coast gunners during the late 1800s and early 1900s. Many islands, coves and marshes afforded nesting and feeding sites for a variety of wildfowl. Chauncey Wheeler became part of this history. He was a riverman, guide and caretaker on the river. When he began hunting he also started carving decoys. His rigs evolved into the magnificent birds the collector sees today. Wheeler is considered the top carver of this region. His elegant reverse feather painting and distinctive eye lines make a Wheeler decoy highly collectible. This brant was found on Long Island, New York. During the 1920s Wheeler made a rig of them for a wealthy family on the island. He also made decoys for John Phillip Sousa and instructed him in carving techniques. Note the tranquil and blue Atlantic Ocean behind this Wheeler brant. A detailed history and photograph of Wheeler can be found in *Decoys Of The Thousand Islands* by Jim Stewart and Larry Lunman and in *Chance*, by Harold Reiser III.

Collection of Harold "Clutch" Reiser III

Canada Goose

by Walter Brady, (1870s-1940s?), Northhampton County, Oyster, Virginia

One of the finest Cobb Island, Virginia, goose decoys was carved and painted by Walter Brady, circa 1890-1910. This decoy merited exposure in William Mackey's book, *American Bird Decoys*, page 157, plate 130. Brady, a Cobb Island guide, oysterman and market gunner was influenced in style by the Cobb family. His geese were sturdy structures. This particular decoy has wonderful lines, an inletted head and the typical split wing and tail carving as seen in Cobb decoys. There are only six to eight known Brady decoys including three brant. Many are repainted and it is therefore rare to find one in such great condition. This photograph was taken at the Ward Museum of Wildfowl Art, Salisbury, Maryland, where the decoy was on exhibit.

Collection of William and Kaye Purnell

Mallard Drake

by Charles "Shang" Wheeler (1872-1949), Stratford, Connecticut

It was a rare privilege to have a special entré to the Dorset House at the Shelburne Museum, Shelburne, Vermont. This is where one of the finest collections of North American decoys is on public display. The majority of decoys were acquired by the museum from the estate of Joel Barber, author of *Wildfowl Decoys* which was published in 1934. His significant collection was amassed during the 1920s through early 1940s and he is considered the father of decoy collectors. This wonderful mallard drake is an important part of the museum collection. Wheeler entered it in the first decoy show in America in Bellport, Long Island, 1923.

A hard look at this work of art tells you quickly who won the blue ribbon, "Shang" Wheeler, of course! Note the turned head attitude and the flowing lines Wheeler constructed. It is difficult to understand why Wheeler would relinquish this decoy to Joel Barber. However, it is fortunate that he did, for Barber cherished it as an important part of his collection. This decoy adorns the dust jacket of *New England Decoys*, by John and Shirley Delph, 1981.

Collection of Shelburne Museum, Shelburne, Vermont

American Widgeon

by Lem (1896-1984) and Steve (1895-1976) Ward, Chrisfield, Maryland

The widgeon is often referred to as the "robber duck" for its habit of stealing food that has been loosened from the bottom by other feeding waterfowl, especially swans with their long necks. Swan confidence decoys are often used in a rig of widgeon decoys for this reason. It was said that Steve Ward considered the widgeon his favorite species. This is evident by the special expression the brothers gave to the widgeon in color and form. In 1928, a Connecticut gentlemen purchased directly from the Ward brothers several decoys including a goldeneye hen, the only known working brant made by the Wards and the widgeon shown here. None of the decoys were ever weighted or used. (Note the insert designating species and maker's name painted on the bottom of the decoy.) In *Ward Brothers' Decoys*, Ronald Gard and Brian McGrath, plate 81, is pictured a similar widgeon decoy from the Bishop's Head Gun Club. It has the same styling as this bird. Both have the typical Bishop head style consistent with the 1928-1933 era. Painted by Lem Ward, this decoy shows his mastery of color and composition. The head is turned and cocked and has the elongated tail consistent with this period. Note the artistic application of flocked paint on the back and sides of this exquisite decoy.

Private Collection

Red-breasted Merganser

by Augustus Wilson (1864-1950), South Portland, Maine

Gus Wilson lived on the rugged coast of Maine all his life. His primary occupations were that of fisherman and lighthouse keeper. Long days and nights at this latter job afforded Wilson the opportunity to carve his now famous lures. He made more than five thousand decoys and sold them to many East Coast hunters which included a large rig of goldeneyes and oldsquaws found on Lake Champlain, Vermont. Wilson's innovative and creative styles make his work collectible, not only to a decoy aficionado but to folk art collectors as well. This merganser is one of three found in a Biddiford Pool, Maine home. Made for this family in the 1920s, it represents the epitome of sculptural beauty. It is worth noting that the red-breasted merganser is the only one of the three forms (the others being common and hooded) of mergansers to be commonly found in salt water.

Collection of James and Patricia Doherty

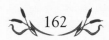

Mallard Hen Sleeper

by Charles Perdew (1874-1963), Henry, Illinois

Charles Perdew, in his early years, traveled the Midwest and eventually settled in Henry, Illinois in 1899. There he began gunsmithing, a bicycle livery, building hunting boats and carving decoys. Between 1917 and 1922, Perdew carved a large rig of decoys for a wealthy banker, G. K. Schmidt, of Rockford, Illinois. For some unknown reason, Schmidt stored them in his bank vault. When they were discovered in the 1960s, Perdew mallards, teals, canvasbacks and Mason decoys saw light for the first time in forty years. They were all in pristine, and for the most part, unused condition. This sleeper decoy was the only Perdew mallard in this configuration. It is unused and branded; G. K. Schmidt. It was painted by Perdew's wife, Edna. Her work is considered to be artistically excellent as this fine decoy illustrates.

Private California Collection

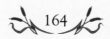

Swan

by Charles Birch (1867-1939), Willis Wharf, Virginia

Charles Birch moved from Chicoteague, Virginia to Willis Wharf in 1906. He became a waterman and had his own oyster grounds, selling his wares to various companies in the East. His focus later changed when he began making fishing boats and 'monitors' which were flat work scows used to ferry equipment from the mainland to the out islands. This ability led Birch to perfect his decoys, making fine sculptured hollow lures. His birds were made in two halves, the bottom being solid to effect ballast and the top half hollowed out; more like New Jersey decoys than the Virginia style. He almost always used iron upholstery tacks for eyes. Birch also made solid decoys but they are considered a lesser quality than the hollow ones. Collectors consider that Birch swans, geese and brant decoys represent his finest effort. This swan decoy, has an oak bill inserted through the head and wedged from the rear. It is photographed gracing the shores of Long Island Sound.

Collection of Alan and Elaine Haid

Canada Goose

by Elmer Crowell (1862-1952), East Harwich, Massachusetts

It is difficult to continually describe Crowell's work in superlative terms. Each of his works seen in this book deserves a poetic portrayal of its beauty. This magnificent goose decoy with its elongated preening head is no exception. It was made circa 1915, has a fluted tail carving and is affixed on the bottom with the oval brand, which reads, "A. Elmer Crowell Decoys, Harwich, Mass." Crowell made this goose decoy, plus two others including a standing variation, for a wealthy Massachusetts family. They eventually found their way in about 1986 to Skinner's Auction House, Bolton, Massachussetts. Prices realized then were world records for Crowell decoys. It was only a short period of time, however, before the asking price for these birds greatly escalated. If you could choose one Crowell decoy to own, this would be it! In January 2000, it was again auctioned and brought a new decoy world record of $684,500. It will be remembered as the highlight of the McCleery collection.

Collection of James McCleery, M.D.
*Private California Collection

Black-bellied Plover

by John Dilley, circa 1885, Quogue, Long Island

Decoy collector and historian Joseph French must be credited with putting a name to the Dilley decoys. Much mystery surrounded these most exquisite shorebirds, prompting French to spend several years researching the Dilley name. In the 1950s, Bill Mackey, noted decoy collector and writer, acquired a rig of shorebirds from the widow of Jess Birdsall. Birdsall was a decoy carver from Barnegat Bay, New Jersey in the 1880s. Mackey referred to the shorebirds as the "Jess Birdsall decoys" in his book, *American Bird Decoys*, published in 1965. French acquired one of these birds. It is pictured here. Although Mackey had alluded to the name Dilley, French traced their origin to Quogue, Long Island. He noted that many of the shorebirds are signed in cursive, "Dilley," below the tail. Besides this decoy, French owns all species carved by Dilley, including a willet pictured in a Milton Weiler painting.

Collection of Joseph and Arleen French

Hooded Mergansers

by Ira Hudson (1876-1949), Chincoteague, Virginia

Chincoteague is an Algonquin Indian word meaning "beautiful land across the water." It was explored and settled by the English in 1670, but not until the Civil War in 1861, did the population begin to increase. The island was a haven for waterfowl and as a result, market gunners began to appear in the late 1870s and 1880s. In 1881, the steamboat "Widgeon" ferried gunners to the island and in 1893 it was the "Lady Ida" hauling out the gunners. Interestingly enough, there is little documentation of any decoy carvers on the island prior to 1900. However, in the early 1900s many noted carvers emerged including Ira Hudson, Dave Watson, Doug Jester and Miles Hancock. The ample magic of the history of Chincoteague Island lured the author there in 1997. Unfortunately, my disappointment was affected by the rampant uncontrolled commercialism that I observed; defying the very definition of the word "Chincoteague." Credit has to be given to Ira Hudson. His decoys personify the definition of the land he loved. The artistic appeal of his decoys is an expression of a focused and ingenious man. This photographed pair of hooded mergansers is certainly one-of-a-kind and is considered to be Hudson's finest work.

Private California Collection

Bishop's Head
Calling Canada Goose

by Lem (1896-1984) and Steve (1895-1976) Ward, Chrisfield, Maryland

The famous Ward Brothers, sons of Travis and Laura Ward, were born in Chrisfield, Maryland, a town on the southeast edge of the Chesapeake Bay. Being brought up with a tradition of gunning and waterfowling gave the brothers an intimate relationship with their environment. Their father, a barber, trained the boys in this profession. However, when hunting created such a demand for their decoys, their fame grew. From practical hunting lures to beautiful decorative pieces, the Ward Brothers could do it all. They made decoys for all the local gun clubs, including the Bishop's Head Club, located south of Cambridge, Maryland. According to Bobby Richardson, author of *Chesapeake Bay Decoys*, the Bishop's Head Club was an exclusive enclave founded in 1923 by Colonel Albanus Phillips from Cambridge, Maryland. He was the owner of Phillips Packing Company, noted for making most of the K rations of World War II. This "Bishop's Head" style of carving occurred after 1923. Many Ward decoys are signed and dated but can also be identified as to era by body conformation. The Bishop's Head style is no doubt the result of an innovative direction by the Wards to identify the decoys with the Bishop's Head Club. The body has a very pronounced apron under the tail, a notch behind the head and a squared off paddle tail.

Collection of Vance and Nancy Strausburg

Canada Goose

by an unknown maker, attributed to Cape Cod, Massachusetts, circa 1890-1905

Even a decoy by an unknown carver has a story. Unfortunately, we cannot resurrect its maker, but only speculate about his obvious talent. This beautifully sculptured goose was one of two in the collection of Stewart Gregory of Wilton, Connecticut. Gregory, a nationally noted folk art collector, had many decoys, most of which were found and purchased for him by Adele Earnest, author of *The Art Of The Decoy*. Gregory considered these geese to be his favorite. Eventually auctioned in 1979 at Sotheby's in New York City, both decoys went to noted collectors, including James McCleery, M.D. At that sale they were hammered down for $10,000 and $12,000. In January 2000, the McCleery goose sold for $235,000, again at Sotheby's. The collector of this goose is convinced it is of Cape Cod origin despite its original designation as being from Pennsylvania. It has a unique structural feature with an interlocking dovetailed union between the neck and the body. The collector also found two shorebirds, a black-bellied plover and a lesser yellowlegs carved by the same maker. All three are pictured.

Private Collection

Widgeon Drake

by John Blair Sr. (1842-1928), Philadelphia, Pennsylvania

John Blair was truly an enigma until noted Delaware River decoy carver and historian, Robert White, solved the mystery. It was initially thought that Blair was a name plucked out of the air; no substantiation of his carving and painting of decoys could be found. However, in 1979, John Blair III, grandson of John Blair, lived in Elkton, Maryland. He quickly resolved many unanswered questions. Blair remembered that his grandfather, a Philadelphia wheelwright, made a rig of mallards just after the Civil War. When asked who painted them, he stated "a trolley painter." This gives credibility to the supposition that Blair Sr. was the carver and his friend was the painter. They apparently worked together painting fine carriages for the Philadelphia wealthy. This very rare decoy is a fine example of the talent of Blair and his friend.

Private Collection

Mallard Hen

by the Caines Brothers, Georgetown, South Carolina, circa, 1890-1900

It is conceivable that the unique style of a Caines decoy was not coincidental. Because of slavery, and a plethora of plantations, many Africans were brought to this area of South Carolina. With them, came their folk art concepts, totally alien and unlike any native to South Carolina. Hence, the Caines could have been easily influenced in this manner and adopted a uniqueness that no other decoy carver in North America can match. During the late 1800s and early 1900s, the Caines were market gunners and worked as guides for the Bernard Baruch family. The Baruch's owned a veritable kingdom; 17,500 acres on the Sampit River just north of Georgetown. Many famous people were guests of the Baruchs: Woodrow Wilson, Grover Cleveland, Winston Churchill and Omar Bradley, to name a few. It is without question that they hunted over Caines' decoys. This photographed "snaky head" mallard hen was purchased privately by the collector. It represents and personifies all that is wonderful in a Caines lure. It is pictured on the edge of a marsh on Fripp Island, South Carolina.

Courtesy of Collectible Old Decoys

Black-bellied Plover

by Obediah Verity (1813-1901), Massapequa, New York

Verity, a descendent of John Henry Verity, was, like his family before him, a market gunner. On the south shore of Long Island, there was a veritable plethora of migratory shorebirds stopping over on their long trek south. Market demands during the 1800s and early 1900s assured the Veritys and other carvers a full-time occupation. Obediah made many species including peeps, dowitchers, curlews, plovers, turnstones and yellowlegs. Tern decoys were also carved as the birds were hunted to provide plumage to the millinery markets of New York City. Fortunately for shorebirds, and unfortunately for Verity, public outcry over the decimation of these unwary, beautiful birds was heard in Congress. By 1918, all shooting of shorebirds was declared illegal. This plover, circa 1885, is in a feeding position and in excellent original condition.

Collection of Alan and Elaine Haid

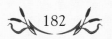

Canada Goose Ice Decoy

by Charles Shoenheider Sr. (1856-1944), Peoria, Illinois

The legend of the geese ice decoys is worth relating. Shoenheider began carving ice ducks in 1910 as part of his market gunning rig. He would use them in conjunction with his floaters. They were ingeniously placed on a partially submerged log which was camouflaged with willow boughs. This was placed near the blind. It was very effective in seducing the wary duck or goose. In 1918, Daniel Voorhees Jr., affiliated with the Duck Island Preserve on the Illinois River, asked Shoenheider to make him a rig of geese. After making a beautiful assembly of twelve ice geese, Shoenheider offered the lot to Voorhees for $125.

Voorhees objected to the price, necessitating Shoenheider to sequester the twelve decoys in his barn. There they remained until 1966. Soon collectors, including Joe French, William Mackey, Adele Earnest, Randy Root and Joe Tonelli, made the decoys part of their cherished American folk art collection. The pictured goose sold for a record price, making the original dozen worth in excess of one million dollars. How about that, Mr. Voorhees?

Collection of James and Patricia Doherty

Hudsonian Curlew

by William Bowman (1824-1906), Old Town, Maine

William Bowman is a name that is relatively new to the decoy collecting community. In the book, *The Art Of The Decoy* by Adele Earnest, page 173, two Bowman shorebirds are illustrated and designated as the work of Elmer Crowell. However, it was up to William Mackey in 1966 to discover the source and history of these very famous shorebirds. Mackey discovered that the Harold Herrick family of Lawrence, Long Island, owned a number of Bowman shorebirds. They related that Bowman, a cabinetmaker and sawmill worker from Maine, would travel each summer to "hunt snipe on the beaches of Lawrence." To substantiate this anecdotal information, several notations in Herrick's diary referred to a Bill Bowman who, "...hunted the marshes on August 21, 1890." This particular curlew is considered the finest Bowman shorebird known. It is very large, measuring eighteen inches end to end and is steel branded T.F. Norton, a gunning companion of Harold Herrick, and has a carved "H" for Herrick. It is on permanent display at The Museums at Stony Brook, Stony Brook, Long Island. It is worth noting that a similar curlew from the James McCleery collection was auctioned in January 2000 for $465,000 and is now an important part of a New Jersey collection.

Collection of The Museums at Stony Brook,
Stony Brook, Long Island

Canada Goose

by Harry V. Shourds Sr. (1861-1920), Tuckerton, New Jersey

When John Hillman, the "Father" of New Jersey decoy collectors, spoke of his collection, he would invariably refer to this hissing Shourds goose as his top decoy. It has been photographed and pictured in five or six books on waterfowl decoys and referred to as one of the finest decoys ever made by Shourds. At auction in 1996, it hammered down at $203,500, the most ever paid for a New Jersey decoy. Harry V. Shourds Sr. set the example for all future Jersey decoy makers. His refined, smooth, hollow and sophisticated lures leave no room for criticism. His output was necessarily prolific to meet the demands of the late 19th and early 20th century market gunners. Tuckerton was a haven for hunters in the 19th century. It has a natural harbor and shipping became an avenue to send barrels of freshly killed waterfowl to the markets of Philadelphia and New York. Many bays and inlets combine to offer migrating waterfowl both brackish and salt water bays from which to feed. Harry V. was up to the demands of this environment and was sought out as the most adept carver on Barnegat Bay.

Private Collection

Swan

by Albert D. Laing (1811-1886), New York City and Stratford, Connecticut

Albert Laing decoys have no equal when it comes to esthetic beauty. Never satisfied with a simple lure, he carved many of his decoys in sleeping positions or with turned preening heads. Any collector would be content to have one decoy with an unusual pose, if it were a Laing. The rarity of an original-paint decoy carved between 1830-1860 is certainly understandable. Used for market gunning, they were often over painted and discarded. "Shang" Wheeler, the most noted early 20th century Stratford carver, often repainted Laing decoys; apparently using them for his own hunting rig. History points to the fact that Laing would travel to the Chesapeake Bay and use his "battery" rig to hunt canvasbacks and other divers. This sleeping swan decoy was used on the bay and found by a noted collector, Quintana Colio, in Chincoteague, Virginia. Its thin body form and bottom board suggest it was a battery decoy used to either shoot swans or as a confidence lure. Note the heavy shot scarring. This decoy dates from the early period, 1830-1840.

Private Collection

Canada Goose

by Phineas Reeves (1833-1896), St. Williams, Ontario, Canada

The Long Point Company, founded in 1866 by a group of seven wealthy Canadian sportsmen, is probably the earliest established gun club in North America. Its original purchase of sixteen thousand acres from the Crown cost fifty cents per acre. It eventually became known as the "Millionaire's Club," with a roster of members such as Cabot of Boston, the Paynes, Winthrops, Whitneys, and Morgans of New York City, as well as Canadian business moguls and British royalty. Reeves was the original club "Punter" or guide for the company. Along with his son John, who was the bookkeeper, Phineas made decoys for the company when he wasn't guiding. George B. Harris, a member from 1877-1896, was the owner of this fine

Phineas-made hollow goose. His initials adorn its side. This is an outstanding example of the carving of the senior Reeves. John left Long Point in the early 1890s to become the head keeper of the St. Clair Flats Shooting Company. All of Phineas' sons, with the exception of Henry, were decoy carvers. They essentially began what is known as the "Toronto School" of carving. Jack Reeves (1904-1986), the grandson of Phineas, was the last of the Reeves to work at the Club. His death in 1986, marked one hundred and twenty years and three generations of Reeves to have guided and hunted at the Long Point Company on Lake Erie.

Collection of Bernard and Martha Crandell

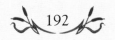

Curlew Decoy

by Nathan Cobb Jr. (1825-1905), Cobb Island, Virginia

Nathan Cobb Jr. is the one son of the Cobb family that is most noted for his decoys. Nathan was a seafaring person and because of the numerous wrecks off the coast, he opened a salvage business. This venture prospered but became secondary to the running of the famous Cobb Island Resort. The issue of logistics; supplies for the tables, ferrying customers from the mainland and entertaining the guests, became paramount. Guiding waterfowl sportsmen and market gunners was also demanding. Nathan supplied the hotel with fresh game as well as shipping barrels of geese, ducks and shorebirds to the northern markets. Nathan Jr. was innovative with his carving techniques. Many of the salvaged ships had seasoned spars of hemlock, cedar or pine, which Nathan used to carve his decoys. Many of the carvings have what is considered the Cobb logo; a deep "N" or "E" (for Elkanah, Nathan's brother), serifed initial in the bottom. This appears predominately on the hollow models and on the swimming and reaching decoys as well as a number of shorebirds. This circa 1885 curlew must personify the expression, "Necessity is the mother of invention." It is presently on exhibit at the Ward Museum of Wildfowl Art, Salisbury, Maryland. At auction it brought the highest price ever paid for a Cobb shorebird.

Collection of Thomas and Cheryl O'Connor III

Mallard Drake

by Victor Alfonso (1899-1982), East New Orleans, Louisiana

Shell Beach, a vast marshy area east of New Orleans, contains large bodies of open water and shallow bays ideal for wintering ducks and geese. Many sportsmen traveled by horse and buggy from New Orleans to hunt divers and puddle ducks. Their primary destination was Lake Borgne. Here Victor Alfonso spent fifty years carving a select number of magnificently sculptured and painted decoys. He was widely known not only as a carver but also as a trapper and a craftsman of cypress dugouts. The mallard pictured here was carved by Alfonso in 1929 as a wedding gift for his wife. Sweeping lines and curves plus a fine patina make this decoy one of Louisiana's finest. This decoy is pictured in *Louisiana Lures And Legends*, Brian Cheramie, 1997, which offers the reader a complete overview of the carvers and the history of this region.

Collection of Brian and Emilie Cheramie

Swan

by John "Daddy" Holly (1818-1892), Havre de Grace, Maryland

The Chesapeake Bay with its vast expanses of marshes and bays has historically been a haven for waterfowl. Great flocks of canvasbacks wintered there. It was here that the famous market gunners would kill thousands of birds for the Baltimore, Philadelphia and New York markets. Resultantly, there was a concomitant demand for working decoys. Members of the Holly family produced thousands of lures for their own use as well as for market gunners and sportsmen. But best known was John, known affectionately as "Daddy." He was recognized as one of the most highly respected duck hunters from Havre de Grace. He often lived full-time with his family on his boat, the William W. Hopkins, fishing commercially and guiding sportsmen. A son, James T. (1849-1935), was also a gifted carver and painter and followed his father's tradition. This swan decoy, no doubt, is the finest example and best preserved of a "Daddy" decoy. Carved circa 1870, it was used either for hunting swans or as a confidence lure. It retains a label from the William Penn Memorial Museum where it was on exhibit in 1964.

Private California Collection

Curlew

by John Henry Verity (1788-1863), Seaford, Long Island

This decoy is the earliest documented shorebird decoy known to exist. John Henry, in his day, was a true legend. As a hunter, carver and guide, his reputation was far-reaching. In the 1844 publication of *Birds of Long Island*, by Jacob P. Giraud, John Henry, affectionately known as "Uncle John," was recommended "to all sportsmen, skilled and unskilled as Uncle John would assist in the marksmanship department to accomplish a full bag." Long Island was a natural stopover for thousands of shorebirds migrating along the Atlantic coast. Therefore, many carvings have originated from this area, including the Eskimo curlew, which was hunted to extinction on Long Island, circa 1860. This curlew, circa 1810-1820, shot scarred on the marshes of Great South Bay, is the prototype for the shorebirds of the "Verity-Seaford School."

Collection of Robert Jr. and Wilma Gerard

Ruddy Turnstone

by Lothrop Holmes (1824-1899), Kingston, Massachusetts

Adele Earnest in her book, *The Art Of The Decoy*, referred to Lothrop Holmes as "the most sophisticated carver of the 19th century." Holmes lived near Duxbury, which was home to many great carvers and to thousands of migratory waterfowl. There is little documentation of the details of Holmes' life and no history that he was a market gunner. It is presumed that the small number of decoys attributed to him were for his own use. Born in 1824, Holmes is one of the earliest recorded carvers in North America. This fact adds to the rarity of his surviving sculptures. This turnstone was part of the Dr. George Starr collection. It was sold in 1986, a year after Starr's death. It realized a price of $67,500, which was a new record for any shorebird. Turnstones are named for their method of feeding. As they walk along beaches, they roll small stones and pebbles to seize prey beneath them. They will also dig large holes in the sand in pursuit of burrowing crustaceans. Turnstone decoys have always attracted collectors and usually demanded high prices. This Holmes decoy is no exception. When auctioned in January 2000, it brought a new world record for a shorebird decoy of $471,000.

Collection of James McCleery M.D.
*Private Collection

Widgeon Drake

by Nathan Rowley Horner (1891-1942), West Creek, New Jersey

If one had to choose the New Jersey Coast or Barnegat Bay decoy icon, it would have to be this very unique widgeon. Some would argue that Harry V. Shourds' hissing goose is at the top. However, there are other geese! This widgeon is one of two and both are part of the same collection. Hollow, with pristine paint and beautifully sculptured form, makes this the rarest of all Horner decoys. Widgeons were seldom hunted in New Jersey and few market gunners bothered with them. Horner was a commercial carver and bayman and made a living selling his decoys. He therefore only made species that were in present demand by hunters. No doubt, a special request prompted him to create these widgeons. This particular species is found mainly on freshwater ponds and bays and will easily decoy into other rigs such as mallards and canvasbacks. Hence, there was little demand and/or need for widgeon decoys, which makes this a truly rare find.

Collection of James and Pat Doherty

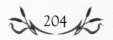

Pintail Drake

by John English (1848-1915) and John Dawson (1889-1959), Florence, New Jersey

This pintail is the most celebrated decoy made by John English and painted by John Dawson. It has attracted attention from both historians and collectors and is considered the finest Dawson paint known. Its picture adorns many books including *Floating Sculpture*, by H. Harrison Huster and Doug Knight. Dawson lived in Trenton, New Jersey, not far from English. When Dawson was in his early twenties, John English died and apparently left many of his hunting rigs to Dawson. English decoys personify all that is both aesthetic and functional in a Delaware River decoy. His mastery of form set the pace for all future Delaware

River carvers. It is interesting that Dawson took such painstaking effort in painting the English decoys, but showed little imagination with his own rig. Fortunately or unfortunately for the collector, Dawson decided to repaint most of the decoys. It's difficult to speculate what a pure English pintail drake would bring at auction. However, we do know about this one. In 1996, the John Hillman collection came up for sale and the pictured decoy sold in excess of six figures. Thank you John Dawson!

Collection of James and Diane Cook

Index

Species of Decoy

A

American Merganser by an unknown maker, 108
American Widgeon by Lem and Steve Ward, 160

B

Bishop's Head Goose by Lem and Steve Ward, 174
Black Brant by William McLellan, 148
Black Duck by Albert D. Laing, 46
Black Duck Sleeper by Robert Elliston, 128
Black-bellied Plover by Elmer Crowell, 98
Black-bellied Plover by John Dilley, 170
Black-bellied Plover by Obediah Verity, 182
Brant by Chauncey M. Wheeler, 154
Brant by Nathan Cobb Jr., 58
Buffleheads by Nathan R. Horner, 152

C

Canada Goose and Pintail Drake by Elmer Crowell, 80
Canada Goose by Captain Charles G. Osgood, 150
Canada Goose by Charles Walker, 52
Canada Goose by Elmer Crowell, 168
Canada Goose by Enoch Reindahl, 122
Canada Goose by George Boyd, 106
Canada Goose by Harry V. Shourds Sr., 188
Canada Goose by Henry Kilpatrick, 88
Canada Goose by Joseph Lincoln, 116
Canada Goose by Nathan Cobb Jr., 96
Canada Goose by Phineas Reeves, 192
Canada Goose by the Warin Brothers, 56
Canada Goose by an unknown maker, 176
Canada Goose by Walter Brady, 156
Canada Goose Ice Decoy by Charles Shoenheider Sr., 184
Canvasback Drake Preener by Elmer A. Crowell, 126
Canvasback Hen by Albert D. Laing, 54
Canvasback Hen by Charles "Shang" Wheeler, 146
Canvasbacks by John Graham, 118
Canvasbacks by Lem and Steve Ward, 44
Curlew by John Verity, 200
Curlew by Nathan Cobb Jr., 194
Curlew by Thomas Gelston, 144
Curlew by an unknown maker, 82

E

Eider Drake by an unknown maker, 136
Eskimo Curlews by the Folger Family, 134

G

Great Blue Heron by an unknown maker, 26
Green-wing Teal by John Blair Sr., 28
Green-wing Teal Drake by Charles Perdew, 114
Green-wing Teals by Elmer Crowell, 92

H

Herring Gull by Harry V. Shourds Sr., 86
Hissing Goose by Nathan Cobb Jr., 66
Hooded Merganser Drake by Orel LeBoeuf, 32
Hooded Mergansers by Ira Hudson, 172
Hudsonian Curlew by William Bowman, 186
Humpback Pintails by Lem and Steve Ward, 8

M

Mallard Drake by Charles "Shang" Wheeler, 158
Mallard Drake by Nicole Vidacovich Sr., 62
Mallard Drake by the Caines Brothers, 84
Mallard Drake by Victor Alfonso, 196

Mallard Drake Ice Duck by Charles Schoenheider Sr., 140
Mallard Hen by Charles Perdew, 132
Mallard Hen by Nathan R. Horner, 142
Mallard Hen by the Caines Brothers, 180
Mallard Hen Sleeper by Charles Perdew, 164
Merganser Drake by Captain Charles G. Osgood, 102
Merganser Drake by Cassius Smith, 74
Merganser Hen by George Boyd, 70
Merganser Hen by John Dawson, 130
Monhegan Island Eider Drake by Augustus Wilson, 42

O

Oldsquaws by Joseph Lincoln, 30

P

Pair of Whimbrels by William Bowman, 78
Pintail Drake by Charles Walker, 60
Pintail Drake by John Blair Sr., 124
Pintail Drake by John English/John Dawson, 206
Pintail Drake by Lem and Steve Ward, 120
Pintail Drake Ice Duck by Charles Schoenheider Sr., 104
Pintail Hen by John English, 138
Pintails by Dave "Umbrella" Watson, 94
Preening Black Duck by Elmer Crowell, 20
Preening Mallard Hen by Robert Elliston, 36

R

Red-breasted Merganser by Augustus Wilson, 162
Red-breasted Merganser by Captain Edwin Backman, 22
Red-breasted Mergansers by Lloyd Parker, 40
Red-breasted Mergansers by an unknown maker, 24
Redhead Drake by Harry V. Shourds Sr., 38
Redhead Drake by Nathan Cobb Jr., 12
Rig of Green-wing Teals by Clovis "Cadice" Vizier, 18
Rig of Mergansers by an unknown maker, 112
Ruddy Duck by Lee Dudley, 50
Ruddy Turnstone by Lothrop Holmes, 202
Running Sickle-billed Curlew by an unknown maker, 64

S

Shorebird Rig by Harry V. Shourds Sr., 72
Short-billed Dowitcher by Obediah Verity, 48
Shoveler Hen by Lem and Steve Ward, 34
Sleeping Swan by Charles "Shang" Wheeler, 16
Snow Goose by John Tax, 76
Swan by Albert D. Laing, 190
Swan by Charles Birch, 166
Swan by John "Daddy" Holly, 198
Swan by an unknown maker, 100

W

Widgeon Drake by John Blair Sr., 178
Widgeon Drake by Nathan Horner, 204
Widgeon Drake by Stevens Decoy Factory, 14
Widgeon Drake Preener by Elmer Crowell, 110
Wood Duck by Thomas Chambers, 10
Wood Duck Drake by Joseph Lincoln, 68
Wood Duck Drakes, Premier Grade, by the Mason Company, 90

Maker

A

Alfonso, Victor, Mallard Drake, 196

B

Backman, Captain Edwin, Red-breasted Merganser, 22
Birch, Charles, Swan, 166
Blair, John Sr., Green-wing Teal, 28
    Pintail Drake, 124
    Widgeon Drake, 178
Bowman, William, Hudsonian Curlew, 186
    Pair of Whimbrels, 78
Boyd, George, Canada Goose, 106
    Merganser Hen, 70
Brady, Walter, Canada Goose, 156

C

Caines Brothers, Mallard Drake, 84
    Mallard Hen, 180
Chambers, Thomas, Wood Duck, 10
Cobb, Nathan Jr., Brant, 58
    Canada Goose, 96
    Curlew, 194
    Hissing Goose, 66
    Redhead Drake, 12
Crowell, Elmer, Black-bellied Plover, 98
    Canada Goose and Pintail Drake, 80
    Canada Goose, 168
    Canvasback Drake Preener, 126
    Green-wing Teals, 92
    Preening, Black Duck, 20
    Widgeon Drake Preener, 110

D

Dawson, John, Merganser Hen, 130
    Pintail Drake, 206
Dilley, John, Black-bellied Plover, 170
Dudley, Lee, Ruddy Duck, 50

E

Elliston, Robert, Black Duck Sleeper, 128
    Preening Mallard Hen, 36
English, John, Pintail Drake, 206
    Pintail Hen, 138

F

Folger Family, Eskimo Curlews, 134

G

Gelston, Thomas, Curlew, 144
Graham, John, Canvasbacks, 118

H

Holly, John "Daddy", Swan, 198
Holmes, Lothrop, Ruddy Turnstone, 202
Horner, Nathan R., Buffleheads, 152
    Mallard Hen, 142
    Widgeon Drake, 204
Hudson, Ira, Hooded Mergansers, 172

K

Kilpatrick, Henry, Canada Goose, 88

L

Laing, Albert D., Black Duck, 46
    Canvasback Hen, 54
    Swan, 190
LeBoeuf, Orel, Hooded Merganser Drake, 32
Lincoln, Joseph, Oldsquaws, 30
    Canada Goose, 116
    Wood Duck Drake, 68

M

Mason Company, Wood Duck Drakes, Premier Grade, 90
McLellan, William, Black Brant, 148

O

Osgood, Captain Charles G., Canada Goose, 150
    Merganser Drake, 102

P

Parker, Lloyd, Red-breasted Mergansers, 40
Perdew, Charles, Green-wing Teal Drake, 114
    Mallard Hen, 132
    Mallard Hen Sleeper, 164

R

Reeves, Phineas, Canada Goose, 192
Reindahl, Enoch, Canada Goose, 122

S

Schoenheider, Charles Sr., Mallard Drake Ice Duck, 140
    Pintail Drake Ice Duck, 104
    Canada Goose Ice Decoy, 184
Shourds, Harry V. Sr., Canada Goose, 188
    Herring Gull, 86
    Redhead Drake, 38
    Shorebird Rig, 72
Smith, Cassius, Merganser Drake, 74
Stevens Decoy Factory, Widgeon Drake, 14

T

Tax, John, Snow Goose, 76

U

Unknown Makers,
    American Merganser, 108
    Canada Goose, 176
    Curlew, 82
    Eider Drake, 136
    Great Blue Heron, 26
    Red-breasted Mergansers, 24
    Rig of Mergansers, 112
    Running Sickle-billed Curlew, 64
    Swan, 100

V

Verity, John, Curlew, 200
Verity, Obediah, Black-bellied Plover, 182
    Short-billed Dowitcher, 48
Vidacovich, Nicole Sr., Mallard Drake, 62
Vizier, Clovis "Cadice", Rig of Green-wing Teals, 18

W

Walker, Charles, Canada Goose, 52
    Pintail Drake, 60
Ward, Lem and Steve, American Widgeon, 160
    Bishop's Head Goose, 174
    Canvasbacks, 44
    Humpback Pintails, 8
    Pintail Drake, 120
    Shoveler Hen, 34
Warin Brothers, Canada Goose, 56
Watson, Dave "Umbrella", Pintails, 94
Wheeler, Chauncey M., Brant, 154
Wheeler, Charles "Shang", Canvasback Hen, 146
    Mallard Drake, 158
    Sleeping Swan, 16
Wilson, Augustus, Monhegan Island Eider Drake, 42
    Red-breasted Merganser, 162